CONTENTS

Acknowledgements

I am indebted to my father, Professor E. H. Warmington, and to Mr. B. H. Polack, who both read the first draft of this book, for many valuable corrections, criticisms and suggestions. My thanks are also expressed to the Trustees of the Colston Research Fund, Bristol. The coins on the cover and frontispiece are reproduced by courtesy of the British Museum.

Bristol, November 1968   B. H. W.

ANCIENT CULTURE AND SOCIETY

NERO
REALITY AND LEGEND

ANCIENT CULTURE AND SOCIETY

General Editor

M. I. FINLEY

Reader in Ancient Social and Economic
History in the University of Cambridge

Other titles in preparation

I

Sestertius (obverse), minted at Rome in 64–66, showing head of Nero with laurel wreath. The legend reads: IMP NERO CLAUD CAESAR AUG GERM P M TR P P P (Emperor Nero Claudius Caesar Augustus Germanicus, *pontifex maximus*, tribunician power, father of his country).

II   III

II *Sestertius* (reverse of I). View of the temple of Janus showing the door closed, with a wreath hung across the top. The legend reads: PACE P R TERRA MARIQ PARTA IANUM CLUSIT S C He closed the temple of Janus after establishing Roman peace on land and sea; by decree of the Senate). Issued after peace with Parthia. (6 cm in diameter.)

III *As* (reverse), minted at Rome in 64–66. Nero as Apollo, with laurel wreath, wearing the traditional robe of a lyre player, and holding and playing the instrument. The legend (continued from the obverse) reads: PONTIF MAX TR P IMP P P (*pontifex maximus*, tribunician power, *imperator*, father of his country). (7 cm in diameter.)

NERO

REALITY AND LEGEND

B. H. WARMINGTON

Reader in Ancient History
University of Bristol

W · W · NORTON & COMPANY · INC · NEW YORK

SBN 393 05397 0   CLOTH EDITION
SBN 393 00542 9   PAPER EDITION

1 2 3 4 5 6 7 8 9 0

MAPS

(Drawn by Denys Baker)

MAIN EVENTS OF
NERO'S LIFE AND PRINCIPATE

All dates are A.D. *except where stated*

ROMAN EMPERORS FROM
AUGUSTUS TO MARCUS AURELIUS

Augustus	31 B.C.–14
Tiberius	14–37
Gaius (Caligula)	37–41
Claudius	41–54
Nero	54–68
Galba	68–69
Otho	69
Vitellius	69
Vespasian	69–79
Titus	79–81
Domitian	81–96
Nerva	96–98
Trajan	98–117
Hadrian	117–138
Antonnius Pius	138–161
Marcus Aurelius	161–180

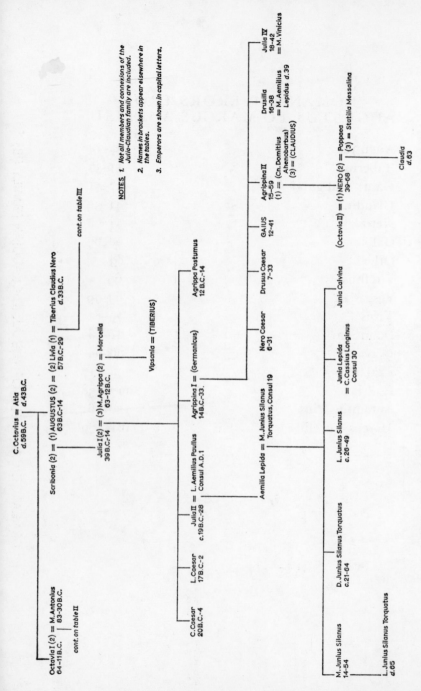

NOTES
1. Not all members and connexions of the Julio-Claudian family are included.
2. Names in brackets appear elsewhere in the tables.
3. Emperors are shown in capital letters.

GENEALOGICAL TABLE OF THE JULIO-CLAUDIAN FAMILY (I)

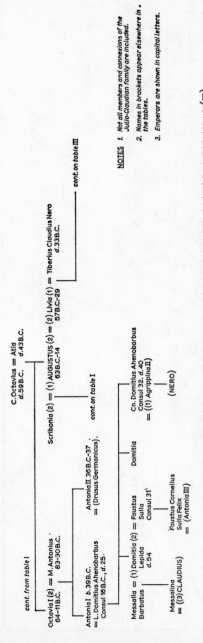

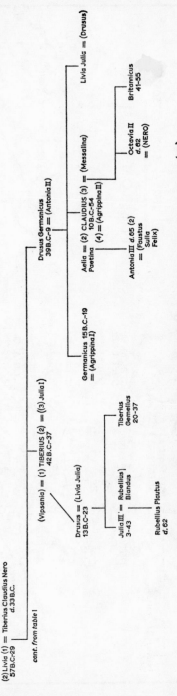

GENEALOGICAL TABLE OF THE JULIO-CLAUDIAN FAMILY (II)

GENEALOGICAL TABLE OF THE JULIO-CLAUDIAN FAMILY (III)

NOTES 1. Not all members and connexions of the Julio-Claudian family are included.

2. Names in brackets appear elsewhere in the tables.

3. Emperors are shown in capital letters.

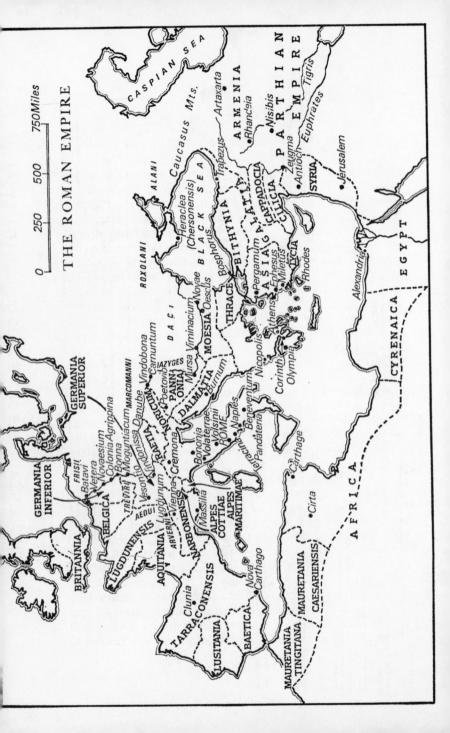

I

Sources for the History of Nero's Principate

HISTORY, it has been said, is the propaganda of the victors, and few better examples could be found to support this view than the history of the Roman Republic and its rise to imperial domination. The Romans' own account of their success is redolent throughout of self-justification; as Gibbon put it, when describing the views of a leading Roman historian, 'according to Livy, the Romans conquered the world in self-defence'. Such history naturally also reflected the interests and prejudices of those under whom Rome had achieved supremacy, namely the senators. These men either wrote the history themselves, or inspired the tradition reproduced by others.

Historical writing remained in the hands of a restricted class even after the establishment of imperial government by Augustus, but the situation was now different because the authority of the Senate diminished rapidly under the emperors. It was more than a century before the senatorial class as a whole became reconciled to loss of power, and in the process there were bitter struggles between it and the emperors, in which the Senate generally lost. Consequently, the history of the emperors from Augustus to Nero (and even later) is rather the propaganda of the victims than the victors. It made little difference if a historian was not a senator by birth, so powerful was the attraction of the senatorial tradition. Recognition of this fact has led generations of modern scholars to try to establish a firmer basis on which to write the history of the Roman Empire. Techniques of source-criticism have given a better idea of the real nature of the ancient sources and of the precise way in which they misinterpreted events and personalities, and have provided means by which some at

1

least of the truth can be disentangled from tendentious comment.

Another problem is that senatorial historians wrote primarily on what went on in the city of Rome, to the neglect of the Empire as a whole. This was perhaps justified when the activities of men of senatorial rank were leading Rome to triumph, but distortion was inevitable when the role of the Senate was diminished under the emperors. There was a concentration on the vicissitudes of the Senate and on the defects of the emperors responsible for senatorial decline. To some extent modern scholarship has been able to correct this imbalance as a result of increased knowledge of the Empire as a whole derived from the study of inscriptions and coins and from archaeology. Understanding of the vast size of the Roman Empire, its relatively primitive economic foundation and its limited administrative structure inevitably diminishes the importance to be attached to the policies, or lack of them, of various emperors, not to mention their private virtues and vices.

The problem of sources is acute for the principate of Nero, who was the object in his own lifetime of anecdotes of the most sensational kind; these have dominated the tradition about him which in one way or another has lasted to the present day. It is true that there are differences in detail between the various accounts, and that one historian or another is more prone to lurid sensationalism, but these are differences of degree; there is no major 'pro-Neronian' element in our sources.

The fact that only one serious treatment of Nero's principate has appeared in this country in a generation seems to show that British scholars have been led by the undoubtedly trivial nature of some of the source material to the conclusion that it was an episode unworthy of the dignity of history. It is hoped to show that this conclusion is unduly pessimistic. Elsewhere, attempts have been made to 'rehabilitate' Nero, but these have really been based on little more than a total rejection of the sources without any supporting evidence; vast and beneficial

2

schemes have been attributed to Nero on the strength of a few favourable anecdotes—the mass of unfavourable ones being rejected. This procedure must be in vain; it is impossible to discredit in its entirety the hostile picture of Nero in the historical tradition, and equally un-historical to reduce the blacks and whites to a uniform grey. It is possible, however, to distinguish between those parts of the tradition which are concerned with matters of some historical significance and those which make little more than light reading. Above all, Nero, the last of his dynasty, must be seen in the context of nearly one hundred years of imperial rule since its establish-ment by his ancestor Augustus, and his personal idiosyncrasies and violent end related to important intellectual and social changes in Rome and Italy.

The earliest extant accounts of Nero's principate date from some fifty years after his death. Cornelius Tacitus, consul in 97 and proconsul of Asia in 112, wrote his *Annals* in the last years of Trajan's principate and the first years of Hadrian's. The surviving books include the principate of Nero from his accession to 66, two years before his death. Tacitus' narrative is the basis of all modern accounts. Besides differences of detail between Tacitus and our other main sources, there are also remark-able similarities, down to verbal identities, which, since it seems established that our existing narratives are in-dependent of each other, must be explained by their common use of narratives now lost. The identification of these lost histories has been the aim of a vast amount of ingenious argument by specialists in source-criticism. The clues are few because, in accordance with the usual practice of antiquity, our surviving authorities rarely indicate their own sources. The subject has its impor-tance, because the lost accounts were all written by contemporaries of Nero.

Early in Book XIII of the *Annals*, which marks the beginning of Nero's principate and of the third and final section of the work as a whole, Tacitus mentions three historians as sources; they are C. Plinius Secundus (generally known as the elder Pliny), Cluvius Rufus and

Fabius Rusticus. He further says that he will abide by his authorities when they agree, naming them only when they diverge. In fact, however, he does not do this; Pliny and Cluvius are mentioned only once more, Fabius twice, though there were certainly numerous occasions when they differed, and Tacitus himself gives some variant versions of events without naming his sources. The reasons for Tacitus' statement and for his failure to abide by it are unknown. The proposed procedure is different from that followed in the first six books of the *Annals*, and a case can be made for the view that the Neronian books were not completed, or lack a final revision in which references to authorities might have been cut out. It is agreed by all scholars that one or more of these three were the main sources of Tacitus and also of Suetonius and Dio, but attempts to identify what each provided are extremely speculative.

Pliny is known from his other writings and from references in the letters of his nephew (the younger Pliny). After an equestrian career he died in the eruption of Vesuvius of 79. Among other works he wrote a history in thirty-one books; the exact period covered is not known, but 41–71 is a possibility. It was written between 69 and 79 but withheld from publication till after his death. It was undoubtedly annalistic in form, chronicling the events of each year, probably one book per year, and thus much longer than Tacitus. From all we know of the author, especially from his surviving *Natural History*, we may conclude that he conscientiously recorded every detail, however trivial, he could lay his hands on; it is most probable that Tacitus means Pliny when he refers (*Annals* XIII, 31) to historians 'who like to fill their pages with praise of the massive foundations and beams of the amphitheatre built by Nero'. (Tacitus names him twice and accepts his word, once without hesitation.) Beyond this, nothing is certain. It has been held that Pliny's account was sober and factual, eschewing the more lurid stories about the court of Nero, to which he seems to have had no direct access, and that one of the reasons for its posthumous appearance was that it

4

failed to vilify Nero in accordance with the general line of historians writing under the succeeding dynasty. But there is much to be said for the view that the author was an uncritical collector of both fact and gossip, that he by no means disliked sensational anecdotes, and that, as an enthusiastic supporter of Vespasian, his account of Nero was thoroughly hostile. The few references to Nero in the *Natural History*, also written and published under Vespasian, are unfavourable and Nero's principate as a whole provided Pliny with a number of examples of ostentatious and useless luxury, one of his greatest bugbears.

Cluvius Rufus was consul at some date before 65, perhaps long before, and was in 'court circles' for much of Nero's principate; he acted as a sort of Master of Ceremonies for the emperor in his appearances in the theatre from at least 65, both at Rome and during his tour of Greece. Nevertheless, he was made governor of Hispania Tarraconensis by Galba; in 69 he supported Otho at first but went over to Vitellius, and he survived the victory of the Flavian cause. In spite of this ambiguous record, Tacitus is not unfavourable whenever he names him; in particular, he attributed to Helvidius Priscus, one of the most outspoken of opponents of imperial autocracy, the remark that Cluvius had done no one any harm under Nero. He also accepts Cluvius' word on the two occasions he is cited as a source. Cluvius, like Pliny, has been held by some to have been Tacitus' major source: he would certainly have had intimate knowledge of court affairs. But nothing is known for certain of the extent or even the form of his historical work. As an expert in the art of political survival, he probably found it prudent in Vespasian's principate to write unfavourably of Nero.

Still less is known of Fabius Rusticus. He was a friend of Seneca, though a generation younger and apparently still living in 108 and known personally to Tacitus. It is not certain that he was a senator. On two of the three occasions he is mentioned by Tacitus his view is rejected, once with the remark that he tended to favour Seneca.

5

Nothing else is known of his work save that it included
something on Britain as well as court affairs and, inevitably, the death of Seneca. Tacitus' remark in the *Agricola*
(10) that Livy was the most eloquent of older historians,
Fabius of the more recent, was a stylistic judgement
implying approval on that score at least. Few have supported the view that Fabius was Tacitus' major source,
but this may be because we know so little; at least some
straw is required for even the most breakable bricks of
source-criticism.

Whether there were other contemporary historians
of the period cannot be known, but is not impossible.
There is also the question whether Tacitus made direct
use of other material. Nero's mother, Agrippina, wrote
memoirs, as did the generals Domitius Corbulo and
Suetonius Paulinus; there were official documents of
two sorts, *commentarii Senatus* (*Proceedings of the
Senate*) and *acta diurna populi Romani* (*Daily Gazette*),
containing miscellaneous items on events in Rome such
as public works, state funerals, important trials and a
summary of senatorial debates; and somewhat later there
were biographies and collections of tracts commemorat-
ing the deaths of those executed by Nero. The answer is
bound to be subjective; was Tacitus the sort of man to
work hard at collating material from archives and minor
literary works not easily accessible before the days of
printing? On the other hand we know from the *Natural
History* and his nephew's account that the elder Pliny
was precisely the man to do all this. It is therefore generally held that the information which can be shown to
have come from such sources was transmitted by Pliny,
and that Tacitus did not consult them directly. This,
however, can hardly be true of the accounts of the deaths
of Nero's victims which were not published before the
principates of Nerva and Trajan. In any case, Tacitus,
as far as we can tell, took little part in public affairs in
the last two decades of his life, and seems to have had
ample time for preparing and writing his historical
works. It is unreasonable to suppose that he did not read
and, more important, evaluate, a variety of material. He

was well aware of the partisan nature of a good deal of historical writing and specifically of the unreliability of much that was written under the Flavian emperors. The view that Tacitus chose one major source and stuck to it is therefore unlikely to be correct, though we may say that the annalistic form of Pliny's work would have provided a suitable chronological basis for Tacitus' own *Annals*, and that its sheer size, implying much detailed information, could mean that it was bound to be the most used. But Tacitus did not merely abbreviate Pliny, reproducing selected material in the inimitable Tacitean style; he was quite prepared to make frequent use of Cluvius and Fabius. It is also probable that he read a lot more, but less probable that he often went to the trouble of referring back to other sources, as it were to check his references. Lastly, it is simply unrealistic to suppose that Tacitus, who was about thirteen on the death of Nero and entered a senatorial career under Vespasian, did not frequently hear details of Nero's principate from his elders, and that such information did not occasionally contradict, or confirm, what was in his sources, and thus affect his own presentation.

As has been mentioned, there are close connexions between Tacitus' narrative and our other surviving sources. C. Suetonius Tranquillus, born about 69, who had a career in the equestrian grades of the imperial administration, rising to the rank of imperial secretary before his dismissal by Hadrian in 121, wrote his *Lives of the Caesars* in the following years. These *Lives* are more like extended journalistic profiles than biographies in the modern sense, yet in their short compass they contain a substantial amount of information. Unfortunately, Suetonius' method of composition in which his material is arranged under various heads such as ancestry, early years, virtues and vices in public and private life and so on, generally without regard to chronology, make the identification of his sources almost impossible. Suetonius' interest was in the emperor in person; thus, in the *Life of Nero* he provides no information about the campaigns in Armenia and Britain since

7

Nero took no part. In reliability he comes far behind Tacitus; even when they can be shown to be using a common source, Suetonius frequently asserts as fact what Tacitus cautiously describes as no more than rumour.

The third main surviving source is Dio Cassius Cocceianus, consul in 222, who wrote a *History of Rome* in Greek. The books covering Nero's principate survive only in excerpts, some fairly substantial, made in Byzantine times. Dio's narrative undoubtedly follows sources available to both Tacitus and Suetonius—he may indeed have used the latter but is far more detailed. His description of the crimes and follies of Nero is sensational, and like Suetonius he often takes gossip and rumour for fact.

A substantial amount of Latin literature other than history survives from the principate of Nero. The surviving works are sometimes informative on aspects of social life and intellectual movements. They must be used with care because of a predominantly moralizing or satirical tone, though this in itself has its significance. The most important are a number of works by Seneca, a few of which, for example the tract *De Clementia* (*On Clemency*), are associated with known political events, while others illustrate the growing importance of Stoic philosophy. As a document of importance in Roman social history, the *Satyricon* of Petronius has an important place for its picture of a Graeco-Roman underworld which barely emerges elsewhere. Its unique character in ancient literature, and other problems, make it difficult to use, however. Alongside the *Satyricon* may be placed a few poems of Martial. In a more conventional manner some minor poets show the optimism with which the beginning of Nero's principate was hailed, while Lucan's unfinished poem on the civil war between Pompey and Caesar seems to reflect the profound disillusionment of the author in Nero's later years. Stoicism, present in Lucan, completely dominates the *Satires* of Persius. Another aspect of Roman life, the traditional devotion to the land, may be seen in a treatise on agriculture by Columella, who died about 65. Columella's practical bent, and an expression of a moral outlook different both from that of Nero's court and of professed philosophers may also be found in the elder Pliny. His vast encyclopaedia of *Natural History*, published a few years after Nero's death, was the result of many years of earlier study.

Outside the Latin sphere, the work by the Jewish historian Flavius Josephus is important, particularly his *Jewish War*. Josephus took part in the Jewish revolt of 66, but went over to the Romans. His account of the revolt is in great detail. As a military historian Josephus frequently compares favourably with Roman writers. Lastly may be mentioned *Acts* and some of the Pauline *Epistles* in the New Testament. Their importance in describing the early progress of an ultimately dominant religion are obvious. When they deal with aspects of Roman law and government they have long been regarded by historians as reliable.

Nero's Accession

ONE of the reasons for the bloodstained character of much of the inner history of the Julio-Claudian dynasty may be found in the lack of an accepted method of succession to the imperial office. This was an inevitable result of Augustus' attempt to disguise the monarchic character of his rule, and avoid the fate of Julius Caesar, by a constitutional fiction that the emperor was not a monarch but *princeps*—Chief Citizen—endowed by the Senate and People with specific legal powers which lapsed with the death of their holder. But it was Augustus himself who tried for over forty years through many disappointments to ensure the succession of one of his descendants. This was not merely due to a wish to perpetuate his power in his family. Sheer political necessity required the continuation of the principate, if the Empire was not to revert to anarchy. A contradiction between the legal characteristics of the principate and a *de facto* hereditary succession were therefore manifest from the beginning. On the other hand there can be no doubt that the idea that the principate should be hereditary was very much stronger than has often been supposed by those historians who have directed their attention to its technical constitutional aspects. The upper classes of Rome and Italy, particularly the senators, many of whom were of great wealth and hereditary influence themselves, were in no position to protest on principle; the transmission of family power and influence from generation to generation had been a major preoccupation of the politicians of the Republic. The idea of a contradiction between 'birth' and 'merit' as qualifications for political power was alien to the Republican tradition and only made itself felt (in a limited way) after bitter experiences at the end of the first century. Members of the ruling class asserted a claim to political power based not only on their own merits but also on the achievements of their ancestors. Thus senatorial objections to the Julio-Claudian succession were due primarily to the monopoly of real power by one family and only secondarily to the accession to the principate of young and untried men like Gaius and Nero.

Among the mass of the ordinary people of Rome and Italy, and the legionary soldiers who were still largely recruited from them, acquiescence in the hereditary principate was complete. The same is true of the provinces, but they did not count as a political factor. Coins of Augustus show that emperor using the means of propaganda open to him to further his dynastic objectives, and inscriptions from various parts of the Empire indicate its effect. At an early stage the imperial family as a whole, and not just the emperor himself, became the object of loyalty:

> 'We swear by Zeus the Saviour, by the deified Caesar Augustus and our Holy Maiden to reverence Gaius Caesar Augustus and all his house . . .' (Smallwood, 33).[1]

At a later date, Tacitus attributes to the praetorian prefect Burrus the statement that his soldiers were loyal to all the imperial family.

The trouble was that there was no fixed or even generally recognized rule of succession within the imperial family. In civil law, Rome lacked almost completely a notion of the importance of primogeniture, a characteristic of medieval feudalism; in general, all a man's sons shared in his estate. So in politics, all descendants of a great man could benefit from their ancestor's renown. Perhaps if Augustus had had a son events would have had a different pattern. As it was, he was forced to turn in succession to his sister's son, his daughter's husband and their sons, and finally his stepson, as he outlived all those he had hoped would succeed. He was ruthless in arranging marriages of a political character

---

[1] References to Smallwood are to E. Mary Smallwood, *Documents Illustrating the Principates of Gaius, Claudius and Nero*, C.U.P., 1967.

for his many female relations (another characteristic of the Republican nobility), even bringing into the scheme daughters of his sister Octavia by his old enemy Mark Antony, besides an impressive number of survivors of noble families. The extent and complexity of the marriage connexions can be seen from the genealogical tables (pp. x–xi). The large number of members who met a violent death indicates the ferocity of the struggles over the succession—and the struggles to maintain power once it was acquired. The importance of the women of the imperial house can also be seen; their marriages were recognized as political events. There was no question of their participation in the principate in any legal sense, but it was only a question of time before one like the younger Agrippina would appear, avid for power behind the scenes as had been some women in the later Republic.

The method adopted for marking out a chosen successor was relatively simple; he would be given various honorific positions and advanced to the consulship far below the minimum ages set for others, and finally given a share in the real powers of the emperor, proconsular and tribunician, so that on the death of the ruler, he would, it was hoped, be in an unassailable position.

Nero was connected with the imperial family on both sides. On his father's, he was a descendant of the Domitii Ahenobarbi, a remarkably lucky noble family which produced eight consuls in eight generations and played a large part in the politics of the Republic. His great-great-grandfather had been an enemy of Julius Caesar and was killed at Pharsalus; his great-grandfather was Mark Antony's most notable supporter and commander of his fleet, though he deserted him at the last moment. This man's son, Lucius Domitius Ahenobarbus, married in 37 B.C. the elder Antonia, daughter of Antony and Octavia. He was consul in 16 B.C. and a distinguished soldier, commanding the armies of Illyria and Germany in arduous campaigns. Nero was said to have inherited all the vices and none of the virtues of the Domitii, and there were

stories of Lucius' cruelty and extravagance, including one
that Augustus had had to cancel a particularly blood-
thirsty gladiatorial show he proposed to put on. Unquestionable loyalty to Augustus and Tiberius seems to have
been a more important characteristic. His son and Nero's
father, Cnaeus Domitius Ahenobarbus, was an equally
deplorable character according to tradition, but he did
well under Tiberius, holding the consulship in 32.
Furthermore, the alliance of the Domitii with the imperial family was strengthened; in 28 he was married to
the thirteen-year-old Julia Agrippina (generally referred
to as Agrippina the younger to distinguish her from her
mother). Their son Lucius Domitius, the future Emperor
Nero, was born at Antium (Anzio) on 15 December 37.

Nero's ultimate accession to the principate was due
above all to his mother, who learned the ways of power
and intrigue at an early age. She, like her husband,
was a descendant of Mark Antony, being the grand-
daughter on her father's side of the younger Antonia.
Vitally important was her descent from Augustus; her
maternal grandmother was Augustus' only child, Julia.
The eldest child of this notorious lady's marriage to the
general M. Agrippa was Agrippina the elder. Her
marriage to Germanicus Caesar produced more children
than any other in the imperial house—nine in all, of
whom six survived infancy.

Germanicus left a reputation throughout the Empire
which was better than that of any other member of the
imperial family except Augustus himself; it is not unduly cynical to attribute this largely to the fact that he
never became emperor. Born Nero Claudius Drusus in
15 B.C., he inherited the name Germanicus on the death
of his father, hero of the German wars. In 4, by order
of Augustus, he was adopted by his uncle Tiberius when
the latter was adopted by Augustus and marked out for
the imperial succession, and in the following years received many honours and commands. The object of
obliging Tiberius to adopt Germanicus when he already
had a son of his own who was very little younger was
to try to ensure the ultimate succession to imperial

13

power of Augustus' own descendants—a notable demonstration of the strength of his feeling. Senatorial tradition
as well as the opinions of soldiers and people were
favourable. Suetonius (*Gaius*, 3) says that 'he possessed
all the noblest endowments of body and mind in a
higher degree than any man before; a handsome person,
extraordinary courage, great proficiency in eloquence
and other branches of Greek and Roman learning besides a singular humanity and a behaviour so engaging
as to captivate the affections of all about him'. Tacitus
on the whole agreed, though indications may be found
of emotional instability, arrogance and theatricality.

Germanicus' death in 19 was generally attributed
to machinations of Tiberius. In subsequent intrigues
over the succession, the widow of Germanicus and his
two eldest sons perished, but in 37 his youngest son,
Gaius Julius Caesar, was in a position to succeed on
the death of Tiberius although he had not been given any
legal powers. The house of Germanicus, which formed
as it were a family within the imperial family, thus
obtained supreme power in spite of its earlier disasters.
One of Gaius' first acts was to have his three sisters,
Agrippina the younger, Drusilla and Julia Livilla, made
honorary Vestal Virgins, and their names were introduced into the formulae for annual oaths taken by
magistrates and soldiers. It was thus in very favourable
circumstances that Agrippina's son was born at the end
of the year. But Gaius lost the initial good will of the
senatorial class within a very short time. A conspiracy
occurred, in 39, the object of which was apparently
to replace him as emperor by his brother-in-law
M. Aemilius Lepidus. Both Agrippina (whose husband
died this year) and her sister Julia were accused of being
in the plot and of committing adultery with Lepidus.
Whatever the truth of the matter the sisters were exiled.

The young Lucius Domitius, whose inheritance was
seized by Gaius, was looked after in the house of his
aunt Domitia Lepida. These difficult circumstances
lasted only a short time. On 24 January 41 Gaius was
assassinated. In the well known episode which followed,

the Senate met and discussed the possibility of 'restoring the Republic'; some members advocated the claims of prominent statesmen, including M. Vinicius, husband of Livilla. But the issue was decided by the praetorian guards. While sacking the imperial palace they discovered in hiding Claudius, brother of Germanicus, and hailed him as the new emperor. The Senate was forced to acquiesce. Claudius, now in his fiftieth year, had been neglected in all previous schemes for the succession because it was believed that he was physically and mentally incapable. In fact some illness or perhaps a spastic condition made him seem uncouth, and he had lived quietly as a scholar on the fringe of the imperial family. When by sheer accident he became emperor, it transpired that he had definite ideas for the use of his power in various fields of policy and administration, particularly in the provinces. But the court was as disturbed as before by dynastic problems, which were exacerbated by the fact that Claudius had neither blood nor adoptive connexion with Augustus. He added the Julian name Caesar, to which he was not entitled, to his own, thus setting it on its way to becoming a title rather than a name.

Agrippina and Julia were recalled from exile and Lucius Domitius recovered his property. He returned to his mother who probably at this date contracted a second marriage, her new husband being C. Sallustius Passienus Crispus, a wealthy middle-aged senator with a high reputation as an orator and wit and a man of much influence. He was given the rare honour of a second consulship in 44. It was perhaps his eminence which protected Agrippina from the emperor's wife Messalina, who procured the exile and death of Julia in 42. Agrippina's wealth was increased when Passienus died (before 47).

It was in this year that the first public appearance of Lucius Domitius, now nine years old, took place. Claudius was celebrating what was considered to be the 800th anniversary of the founding of Rome with a special festival called *Ludi Saeculares*. Included in the celebrations was a traditional pageant about the siege of

Troy, performed by young nobles. Domitius and Claudius' son Britannicus, only six years old, took part, and the former was greeted with popular enthusiasm owing to the memory of Germanicus, of whose formerly extensive family Lucius and his mother were now the last survivors. Popular sympathy was said to have been increased by the hostility of Messalina, but legend rather than fact is all that is known about alleged danger to Domitius.

Opportunity for Agrippina and her son came with the execution of Messalina in 48. The recorded details of this event, as Tacitus and even Suetonius admit (*Annals* XI, 27; *Claudius*, 29), are almost incredible, but there seems to have been a plot to replace Claudius as husband of Messalina, and as emperor, by the consul designate C. Silius. Claudius swore that he would never marry again (Messalina was his third wife) but soon changed his mind. It was said that he was incapable of living without a wife, though he had two well-loved concubines, but political considerations played a part. The court was torn by competing interests. Some favoured the cause of Aelia Paetina, Claudius' divorced second wife, others that of Lollia Paulina who had been Gaius' third wife. Agrippina had the support of Pallas, one of Claudius' most influential freedmen, and her descent from Augustus (and Germanicus) was probably the decisive factor in her victory. The fact that Claudius was her uncle and that such a marriage was incestuous in Roman law was easily disposed of by senatorial decree, and the marriage took place at the beginning of 49.

Claudius' daughter Octavia, now ten years old, had earlier been betrothed to L. Junius Silanus, a great-grandson of Augustus. Like the marriage of Claudius to Agrippina, this match also was intended to link the house of Claudius with that of Augustus; although the Silani were of much less importance than the family of Germanicus, they continued to be regarded as potential successors because of their descent from Augustus, and were finally destroyed. By 48, Silanus, now about twenty-two, was in a strong position if Claudius should die, since Britannicus was too young to succeed. He had been with Claudius on his expedition to Britain and launched on the traditional offices long before the statutory minimum age. Even before her own marriage, Agrippina had determined to destroy him and thus leave her son as politically the most suitable husband for Octavia. One of Claudius' most influential senatorial advisors, L. Vitellius, charged Silanus with incest with his sister, Junia Calvina; Claudius broke off the betrothal, while Silanus was expelled from the Senate and forced to lay down his praetorship. He committed suicide on the day of Claudius' marriage. Other supporters of Agrippina procured a decree of the Senate asking Claudius to betroth Octavia to Lucius Domitius and this was done. In the same year Seneca was recalled from exile, designated for the praetorship and made tutor to the boy (see below, p. 26).

Agrippina's next success was to get Claudius formally to adopt her son. The precedents advanced were Augustus' reliance on his stepsons Tiberius and Drusus during the youth of his grandsons (and adopted sons) Gaius Caesar and Lucius Caesar. This was hardly relevant, since Tiberius was not adopted (at this stage) by Augustus. The other was the adoption of Germanicus by Tiberius, though he had a son of his own. Nevertheless the adoption took place on 25 February 49; Lucius Domitius Ahenobarbus became Tiberius Claudius Nero Caesar, though this official designation was almost immediately and generally replaced by Nero Claudius Caesar Drusus Germanicus. Later in the year Agrippina was given the title Augusta, the first wife of an emperor to bear it in her husband's lifetime.

In 51, before his fourteenth birthday, Nero assumed the *toga virilis*, the adult dress which indicated his majority, and he was now able to enter public life. The Senate decreed that he should be consul in his twentieth year and meantime enjoy proconsular power outside Rome. He became *Princeps Iuventutis* (Leader of the Youth)—an honorary position of head of the young nobility—and a supernumerary member of the four traditional colleges of priests. Such honours exceeded what had been done for any young member of the imperial family since Gaius and Lucius Caesar and were reflected at once in the imperial coinage. Gifts were made in his name to the soldiers and the Roman people, and the contrast between Nero at the Games in triumphal robe and Britannicus still dressed as a child was obvious. Agrippina secured the dismissal of the latter's tutors, and it is said that officers of the praetorian guard who were sympathetic to him were removed, or promoted to provincial posts; finally the praetorian prefects Lusius Geta and Rufrius Crispinus, whom Agrippina believed loyal to Messalina's children, were replaced. It is not certain that political considerations were apparent in every case; at any rate Geta became prefect of Egypt, a post in which unquestionable loyalty was the first consideration. There was a disciplinary argument (used by Agrippina) in favour of putting the praetorians under one commander; the new man was Sextus Afranius Burrus.

Nero's marriage to Octavia took place in 53 and in the same year he made a number of appearances in the Senate. Before this he is recorded as having spoken there in 51 when he thanked Claudius for his various honours, and in 52 when he vowed to give games for the recovery of Claudius from illness. His speeches in 53 were on behalf of a number of communities in the Empire. Presumably they were written for him by Seneca (see below, p. 27) but it is notable in view of Nero's later enthusiasms that three were in Greek. Naturally all Nero's petitions were successful; Ilium (Troy) received privileges in the form of exemptions from public burdens to add to those she already enjoyed in virtue of her legendary past; the island of Rhodes, whose free status had been revoked some years before, again became formally free for a brief period; Apamea in Syria received immunity from taxes for five years because of damage from an earthquake. In Italy, Bononia (Bologna) received a grant of ten million sesterces to help recovery from a fire.

However, the position of Nero was not unassailable. Just as court and Senate had had factions in similar situations under previous emperors, so now we can catch glimpses, though no more, of a group which favoured Britannicus. In particular, Claudius' most influential freedman, Narcissus, was loyal to his cause. The Senate itself found the strength to expel an unpopular member though it was known that he was a supporter of Agrippina. The latter found it necessary to attack Nero's aunt Domitia Lepida. It was said that she had tried to win Nero's affection by spoiling him, but in view of the fact that she was supported by Narcissus, it is probable that her relationship with Britannicus was the trouble— she was his grandmother. Domitia was condemned to death on charges of plotting against Agrippina. Nevertheless there were signs that Claudius was preparing to re-establish Britannicus, probably when he reached the age at which Nero had been given adult status; he would be fourteen on 12 February 55. Suetonius (*Claudius*, 43) relates that Claudius said he would do this 'so that the Roman people may at last have a real Caesar'. Even if only gossip, this would indicate an important fact; the prestige of the house of Germanicus and the general acceptance in Rome of adoption for political reasons were not sufficient to make the passing over of Britannicus wholly acceptable to public opinion. He was the first son of an emperor in a position to succeed. A rare coin (Smallwood, 105b), with the portrait and title of Britannicus, and some other coins and inscriptions in the provinces show the continuing interest in Claudius' son.

Claudius died suddenly on 13 October 54. Contemporary writers soon had the whole story, with a number of substantial variations, but all describing in some detail the poisoning of the emperor at the instigation of Agrippina. The versions are reproduced in our main sources. Only Josephus regarded the story of poison as a rumour. The most popular version, that mushroom was the vehicle of the poison, obviously has the possibility of a misinterpreted accident, and Nero's repeated joke that mushroom was the food of the gods is no evidence either way, though contemporaries thought it was. The elder Pliny happens to record the death a few years later of Annaeus Serenus, Prefect of the Watch, along with a number of his centurions and tribunes, by accidental poisoning by venomous fungi. It may be noted as illustrative of the precautions observed by the emperors that the office of imperial food-taster, a palace servant referred to in the story of the death of Claudius, already existed under Augustus. On the other hand the death of Claudius came at such an opportune time for Nero that the tradition has generally been accepted.

While the children of Claudius were detained in the palace, Nero appeared outside with Burrus. He was hailed by the unit of guards on duty and taken to the praetorian barracks. Some soldiers asked for Britannicus, but no reply was made. After the promise of 15,000 sesterces per man (the same donative had been given by Claudius), Nero was hailed as *imperator*. Only then did he go to the Senate House to receive all the powers and honours which had been enjoyed by previous emperors, refusing only the title 'Father of his Country'. Claudius' will was not read; Dio and Suetonius imply that it favoured Britannicus, but it may be supposed that there was no solid information available, and that their view was a simple deduction from the will's suppression. Tacitus characteristically deduced the opposite; the will is said to have put Nero first and was suppressed in order to divert popular feeling that Britannicus was being unfairly treated. The question of the will was not unimportant; Tiberius had named Gaius and his own grandson Tiberius Gemellus joint heirs and the Senate had set the will aside because of a definite feeling that despite all legal theory, the emperor's choice of heir to his property indicated his choice of successor to his power, whereas in fact Gaius had seized sole power and excluded Tiberius Gemellus. Hence the suppression of Claudius' will implies at least the equality of the two boys.

3

Seneca and the Principles of Government

OVER eighty years had passed since the day in January
27 B.C. when C. Julius Caesar Octavianus laid down the
extraordinary powers by which he had been ruling the
Roman world and, to use his own words, 'transferred
the Republic from (my) own power to that of the Senate
and People of Rome' (*Res Gestae*, 34). The constitutional devices through which, now under the name of
Caesar Augustus, he not only retained but extended his
personal power need not be detailed here. They were
so ingenious and so effective that formal changes under
later emperors during nearly two centuries were unimportant. They enjoyed from the beginning of their
principates the powers which Augustus accumulated
over a period of time—in particular, proconsular power
over the largest and militarily the most important provinces, tribunician power, and the chief priesthood. The
division of the Roman Empire between so-called imperial
provinces whose governors (*legati Augusti pro praetore*
of senatorial rank in most cases, with a few provinces
allotted to men of equestrian rank) were appointed
directly by the emperor, and senatorial provinces whose
proconsuls were chosen by lot from senior ex-magistrates,
continued, but the distinction became increasingly
formal. By the time of Nero all the legions and almost
all auxiliary units were in the imperial provinces and in
any case all soldiers took their oath of allegiance to the
emperor. The latter was entitled to intervene in or
legislate for all provinces alike. In Rome itself the ancient
magistracies continued, but their activities were increasingly confined to judicial business in the city and in
Italy.

The most important developments since Augustus
were in the realities of power, not in changes of form. It
could certainly be held for a while that traces of true

Republicanism survived, especially since Augustus often preferred to use his overwhelming prestige (*auctoritas*) to have his ideas put into effect rather than formally to legislate himself. But the ease with which Rome and Italy accepted an autocracy only faintly disguised is remarkable. The emperor Tiberius is said to have been disgusted at the way in which the Senate, the body which should have manifested the traditions of the Republic, showed itself increasingly servile, and the theme is a constant one in Tacitus. The reasons given for this are no doubt correct—the civil wars and disorders of the late Republic were destructive of life and property in Rome and Italy, and were seen to be likely to destroy the Roman Empire itself; only firm control by one man could maintain peace, and so it proved. Over forty years of generally successful rule by Augustus did as much as anything to justify his whole system; when he died there was no one left who could remember from his own experience how the old Republic had actually worked. His concessions to Republican forms were sufficient to win the acquiescence of the upper class in Rome and Italy as a whole, though there were exceptions. This class, through the Senate and equestrian order, provided the traditions and experience in government required by Augustus for the running of the Roman Empire.

There was a price to be paid, and it was not small. The contradiction between the fact of a government monarchical in all but name, and the theory that Republican government, and especially the supremacy of the Senate, survived, led to tensions between some emperors and the upper class which poisoned the atmosphere in Rome and Italy. It was useless for emperors such as Claudius to urge the Senate to behave as a Senate should, while at the same time increasing his own direct control over affairs. This contradiction was the so-called 'lie of the Principate'. Augustus himself possessed or could easily have acquired the powers of emperors later regarded as tyrants; what mattered was the way in which the emperor used his powers. The

Augustan principate was generally agreed to represent the standard by which his successors should rule, but this was useless; so much depended on the personal approach rather than forms, that within a generation of his death no one could know what the reality had been. Tiberius tried to follow closely, perhaps too closely, the 'precepts of Augustus', but he had little gift for the pretences which Augustus had kept up. Gaius in his turn knew of nothing but imperial rule, and saw the possibilities and the pleasures of undisguised absolutism.

The principate of Claudius brought more trouble. The Senate, it might be said, was bound to be in difficulties with a ruler like Gaius whose approach was irresponsible, but Claudius, with an undoubtedly sincere feeling for the spirit and traditions of the Republic, was surely differ-- ent. Furthermore, the number of noble families whose traditions of active power went back to the Republic was by now negligible; the Senate consisted to a large extent of wealthy Italians who were the first of their families to enter it, or at any rate whose rank went no further back than Augustus. It became plain, however, that the 'new men' recruited generation after generation from the equestrian order into the Senate were liable to feelings of nostalgia for the Republic. Although the great majority willingly acquiesced as individuals in imperial rule, resentment at any real or imagined slight to the Senate's prestige was easily roused. This affected their attitude to Claudius. This emperor, it transpired, in spite of his undistinguished past and the comic way in which he had been thrust into the imperial position, positively enjoyed the activity of government. He immersed himself in day to day judicial business, very probably to the detriment of larger concerns, and was active in responding to issues raised particularly in the government of the provinces. It was not that he had a vast plan of reforms for the Empire—no Roman statesman except perhaps Julius Caesar ever had—but as problems and requests were presented to him he responded in a way which could generally, though not always, be described as reformist. But the increase in the emperor's activity and his assumption of personal responsibility in fresh fields led to importance being acquired by his personal assistants, at the expense of Senate and knights.

All his predecessors, including Augustus, had had a staff of personal secretaries and assistants drawn, as the custom was in noble Roman houses, from their own slaves or freedmen, many of Greek origin. It is often loosely said that Claudius created a centralized bureaucracy or even a civil service, and ancient sources are unanimous that the freedmen of the emperor vastly increased their power under Claudius. In form he may have done little more than allot clearly defined functions and establish special offices with larger staffs under chief secretaries. We know in particular of his chief private secretary (Narcissus by name), chief accountant (Pallas), judicial secretary (Callistus) and cultural secretary (Polybius). The effect was that what was in law the emperor's private household became in fact the central executive office of a large part of the imperial administration. It was quite clear that important decisions would in practice be made by the imperial freedmen, and that this would increase imperial control over officials of both senatorial and equestrian rank. In one sense the latter had only themselves to blame; till the end of the century it was considered socially unacceptable for men of free birth to hold such secretarial positions, however responsible.

Tradition was unanimous that Claudius was dominated by his wives and freedmen, but this has been disputed by modern writers. The envy and resentment of the senatorial and equestrian orders at the power and wealth of a socially despised group is manifest. Yet it is notable that although the importance of the freedman element in the administration continued to the end of the century, no other emperor is portrayed like Claudius. Many freedmen of importance are known by name from the principate of Nero, and their influence is on specific occasions attested; for example, Polyclitus, sent to Britain to settle a dispute between governor and procurator, and Helius, left in charge at Rome when Nero visited Greece. Yet for all the hostility shown to Nero, it is not alleged that he was dominated by them. The fact seems to be that Pallas, Narcissus and the rest really did enjoy more power, and acquire more wealth, than any other freedmen known to us. This may not show that Claudius was dominated by them, but does indicate that he listened to their advice as often as to his senatorial councillors, and turned a blind eye to their spoils of office. There was perhaps a vicious circle here. Claudius, unsuccessful in obtaining the co-operation of the upper classes yet determined to increase his personal role, turned to his household officials, which only aroused more resentment. There is a useful analogy with certain medieval rulers whose difficulties with their feudal subjects were ·often attributed to the influence of unworthy favourites. To deny the power and influence of the freedmen would be to fall unconsciously into the same error as Claudius' detractors, that freedmen were the wrong sort of people to advise an emperor. No doubt their profits were enormous, but profits (in moderation, it was hoped) were expected from all posts in the administration (see below, p. 59). They certainly worked harder and were more professional than the senatorial, if not the equestrian officials, with their amateurism and tradition of dignified leisure; and it may be supposed, though it cannot be proved, that the complaints and requests of provincial communities would be not less favourably received by them than by men of the Roman and Italian upper class, still frequently indifferent to the claims of the subjects of the Empire.

Many senators and knights had lost their lives under Claudius both as victims of intrigues at court and as the result of tensions between the emperor and the two orders. It could be hoped that the young Nero, only seventeen on his accession, would follow a different path, whether as a result of his own personality and upbringing or, in view of his own inexperience, a willingness to be guided by advisers sympathetic to the ideas of the Senate. His tutor Seneca hoped that his book *De Clementia* (*On Clemency*), which he dedicated to Nero in 55, 'would serve as a mirror in which you may see yourself' (*De*

Clementia I, 1). There was an established body of Hellenistic theory on the duties of kingship, but little in the Roman tradition to serve as a 'Mirror of Princes'. The education of Nero had followed the normal pattern for the children of Roman nobles up to the time of Agrippina's marriage to Claudius. It was in the hands of Greeks, both free and freedmen. The names of the boyhood companions with whom he shared his teachers (for he was certainly not taught alone) are not known. His earliest teachers were Beryllus, a Greek of Palestinian Caesarea, and Anicetus, a freedman who later became prefect of the fleet at Misenum, and notorious for his part in the deaths of Agrippina and Octavia. Later we hear of a certain Alexander of Aegae, a philosopher of the Peripatetic school, and Chaeremon, a notable Stoic and leader of the intellectual community of Alexandria. Chaeremon had been on an important mission sent by the Alexandrians to Claudius in 41. He was the author of a history of Egypt, and books about hieroglyphs and about comets. These diverse interests, so characteristic of the period especially among Stoics and those influenced by them, may have brought him to the notice of Seneca when he was in Egypt. Seneca's appointment as Nero's tutor was something of a novelty though Romans of the upper classes at a somewhat higher age were increasingly being sent to teachers of rhetoric and philosophy who were Roman citizens rather than Greeks.

 Nero had a lively mind, and in addition to his artistic interests in carving, painting and above all music, pursued a course of study which was wide-ranging if not profound. 'He applied himself to almost all the liberal disciplines, but his mother diverted him from philosophy as an unsuitable subject for one destined to become emperor.' (Suetonius *Nero*, 52.) This was not so much a snub to Seneca as evidence of the attraction which philosophy had for the young at this time, and of the prejudices against it; Seneca's own early enthusiasm had been considered excessive, and in a situation curiously parallel to Nero, Tacitus' father-in-law Agricola had when young been addicted to philosophy 'more than was fitting for a Roman and a senator', and been rescued by his mother. Seneca's duty was undoubtedly to teach Nero the art of rhetoric, and to provide worldly advice on imperial behaviour. It was said that Seneca discouraged Nero from reading orators of an earlier age in order to secure his devotion to himself, but this looks tendentious. Nero, who adopted all the fashionable attitudes of his time, will have needed little inducement to follow the style of Seneca, so pervasive and popular among a whole generation of Romans. Tacitus went so far as to imply that Nero, unlike his predecessors, never obtained proficiency in the art of speaking and regularly had his speeches written for him by others; this was felt to be a serious deficiency in an emperor. However Tacitus seems to have exaggerated, though it may be the case that Nero simply disliked making formal speeches. Nero probably acquired from Seneca an interest in natural phenomena such as was shown in his expedition to discover the source of the Nile, or his attempt to sound the depth of Lake Alcyon during his visit to Greece.

Seneca is said to have had early forebodings of Nero's cruelty but this was perhaps wisdom after the event. It will be seen that Seneca and his friends had little to complain of for a number of years. Judgement on how far Nero was acting autonomously or under the advice of others during the first part of his principate must be subjective; ancient writers were always ready to see hidden influences at work. Thus, since it was the general view that Nero was vicious and cruel from the start, the relatively good beginning to his principate had to be explained by his lack of interest and by the efforts of his advisers. Dio stated roundly (LXI, 4) that 'Seneca and Burrus took the government into their own hands and administered affairs in the best and fairest way they could, with the result that they were equally praised by everyone.' His view, or that of his sources, was that Nero was basically not interested in public business and preferred to indulge in his private pleasures while allowing the government to be carried on by others. Tacitus is not so direct but is in substance in agreement, and indeed most of the evidence favours this view. Nero was not like his ancestor Augustus, dedicated to the pursuit of supreme power from the age of eighteen. His personal activity in affairs is certainly attested on a number of occasions, and we read of discussions with his advisers, but the fact is that the emperor's direct participation in business could not be reduced below a certain minimum. In particular, judicial business took up much time, appointments to high positions needed care, as did the military problems of the time, and there were always documents for signature. Within these activities, there was scope for the well attested examples of Nero's extravagant and unrealistic ideas, sometimes of a sentimental kind, which, however, he was willing to be talked out of. Nevertheless, it is clear that Nero's concern with public business was spasmodic, and that Seneca and Burrus were the men largely responsible for the day to day running of affairs for some eight years.

This influence was exercised primarily in the emperor's *consilium* (private council), not in the Senate; Seneca is never shown in a senatorial context. The confidential nature of the proceedings in the *consilium* of all emperors was such that we know little of its inner history. We cannot often trace the interplay of interests and personalities or estimate the authority of individual members. In the case of Nero, the whole tradition represents Seneca and Burrus as having the real power, though the *consilium* certainly included a number of other members. Opinions differed as to which of the two was the more important. Tacitus uses the order Burrus and Seneca, and says that it was the death of Burrus which broke Seneca's power. This judgement does not, however, imply that Burrus was the dominant influence on public business. It is inconceivable that the good relations between Nero and his advisers on the one hand and the Senate on the other could have subsisted with the dominant influence being the praetorian prefect, an equestrian. The maintenance of these good relations was a notable achievement and one which must be due to the talent of Seneca for working both with Nero and the

Senate as a body. Tacitus describes the relationship between Burrus and Seneca (*Annals* XIII, 2): 'They enjoyed a unanimity rare in partners in power and were equally influential by different methods. Burrus' influence was in military efficiency and in integrity of character, Seneca's in his teaching of eloquence and in his affability combined with dignity.' In fact, Tacitus overestimates Burrus as a military man; he never rose above the military tribunate in the army till he became praetorian prefect, and had spent most of his career as a procurator (financial agent) of Livia, Tiberius and Claudius. Such experience in finances and administration was useful—Seneca too had financial talents. Nevertheless, control of the praetorian guard was important, and when Burrus died in 62 and was succeeded by Faenius Rufus and Tigellinus, who was hostile to Seneca, the latter felt that his chief support was gone.

Burrus was born at Vasio (Vaison) in Gallia Narbonensis; Seneca came from Corduba (Cordova) in Baetica. Thus two provincials were at the heart of affairs. Seneca was, it seems, the older man, being born about 4 B.C., the second of three sons of a wealthy rhetorician. The sons, all of whom obtained some eminence, were brought up in Rome, and Seneca proved an outstanding pupil of his father and of other rhetoricians. His chief love was, however, philosophy, and his youthful enthusiasms were such that he became a vegetarian on Pythagorean principles, and practised austerity under the influence of Stoicism. His health was affected by his excessive zeal and he visited Egypt for convalescence. (His aunt was the wife of the prefect.) One of his earliest works was written then, on the religion of Egypt. He returned to Rome about 31 and obtained the quaestorship, well above the normal age because of his long absence, and began his career as an advocate. In the next ten years his success must have been enormous, though we know little about it. He is said to have aroused the antagonism of Gaius who called his style 'sand without lime'. But this style, elusive and insinuating, became the model for an entire generation of educated Romans, in reaction from the rounded formalities of the Ciceronian style. Not just his literary merits but a personal charm seem to have made him acceptable in the highest circles. At any rate, shortly after the accession of Claudius, he was exiled to Corsica on a charge of adultery with Gaius' sister Julia. It is possible that this was due to Messalina, eager to attack the members and friends of the house of Germanicus, and his subsequent recall in 49 by Agrippina shows that he was indeed an associate of this group.

In his appointment as tutor to Nero and still more in his emergence as a decisive influence in 54 we have evidence of a political talent and of a personal charm and capacity for winning support which seem to be summed up in Tacitus' reference to his affability and dignity; in terms of normal Roman politics his connexions with other influential persons were negligible. His qualities as a man of affairs may now be detected in only a few of his letters, and if our failure to grasp them is due to differences in taste and attitude between our day and his, it may be observed that later generations of Romans found him an easy target for criticism. Seneca laboured under a double disadvantage—a philosopher who became a millionaire, a moralist who was Nero's closest adviser. Such criticisms were the easier to make since the positive side of Seneca's political activity, exercised as it was in the *consilium*, was concealed from view in any detail, and his own writings of a later date were almost totally discreet. The relatively generous treatment of Seneca by Tacitus may therefore have weight. The historian had the keenest of eyes for hypocrisy, yet did not charge him with it. He knew well enough the accusations that could be made against Seneca, in particular a notable talent for making money, but never criticized him directly. This is in contrast with his treatment of, for example, L. Vitellius, the ruthless adviser of Claudius, and Eprius Marcellus, notable later in Nero's principate as a prosecutor in treason trials. Seneca, it seems, was one of those who, though in one sense servants of a tyrant, nevertheless did the best they could, and in particular did not abuse their power to injure others. In Tacitus' pessimistic view of what was to be expected under autocrats, this was to be commended.

The first political action of Nero's principate was the deification of Claudius, the first emperor to receive the honour since Augustus. This measure was an inevitable consequence of the power of Agrippina in the previous years. On the coinage of the last years Claudius she and Nero both appear with increasing frequency, and it was clear that the claim of Nero to the imperial position was based not only on his descent by blood from Augustus but also on adoption by Claudius. It was likely to appeal to the army, to which Claudius had been attentive, and to the provincials, many of whom had undoubtedly benefited from his measures. Although the Senate had in effect posthumously condemned the memory of Tiberius and Gaius by not deifying them, the tendency to bestow quasi-divine honours on emperors even in their own lifetime was such that Claudius' deification could cause no affront to traditionalists. The event was referred to on imperial coinage of 54 and 55 and a temple in his honour was begun by Agrippina, though it was afterwards neglected by Nero and only completed by Vespasian. References to 'Divus Claudius' were dropped from the coinage in 55 when the disadvantages of the deification became apparent (see below, p. 45) but remained, inevitably, in the official nomenclature of Nero, which ran as follows:

> Nero Claudius Caesar Augustus Germanicus, son of the deified Claudius, grandson of Germanicus Caesar, great-grandson of Tiberius Caesar Augustus, great-great-grandson of the deified Augustus.

This formidable genealogy which linked Nero with three previous emperors, omitting only the lamentable Gaius, was most significant. According to Roman practice, after mentioning his (adoptive) father Claudius, it should have run 'grandson of Drusus Germanicus', i.e. the father of Claudius. This was omitted and the descent through his mother from Germanicus and thus from

31

Tiberius and Augustus substituted. The irregular nomenclature was retained even after the death of Agrippina and demonstrates the importance of Nero's membership of the Julian family.

Seneca wrote the speech which Nero delivered at Claudius' funeral, and speeches on later occasions as well. The funeral speech was laudatory and unimportant; that delivered by Nero in the Senate House on the same day gave the aspirations of the new government. Nero promised to govern according to the principles of Augustus, and rejected practices which had caused resentment under Claudius—the emperor's sitting in judgement in private, the corruption of his court and the identification of his household with public administration. The privileges of the Senate and its competence in Italy and the senatorial provinces were assured.

Such well-intentioned speeches were the common form of the first and second centuries particularly if an effective but not too discrediting contrast could be made with the last ruler. The initial programme of Gaius is known to have been in a similar vein, and the resulting disillusionment might have been a warning. However, the Senate enthusiastically voted to have the speech inscribed in gold and publicly read in the Senate at the entry into office of the new consuls at the beginning of each year. There can be no doubt of the generally enthusiastic welcome. Several contemporary poets hailed the new régime in terms reminiscent of those used in the age of Augustus, stressing in particular the theme of universal peace, and as late as 60 or 61, Lucan, nephew of Seneca, published what amounted to a panegyric on Nero in the first book of the *Pharsalia*: 'If fate could find no other way for the advent of Nero . . . we complain no more against the gods; even such crimes and such guilt (i.e. the civil wars of 49–45 B.C.) are not too high a price to pay.' (I, 33ff.) Seneca's *De Clementia*, completed in 55, amplified the ideas which he hoped Nero would follow. By clemency he did not mean a sentimental policy of excessive generosity and the overlooking of all offences, but a general benevolence which would include the qualities expected of a good ruler, basically in accordance with the long tradition of Hellenistic, largely Stoic, writing on the duties of kingship. What is remarkable in the work, however, is the way in which Seneca exalted the power of the emperor. All depends on him; his power is effectively absolute, and subject only to his own conscience. This was no doubt due in part to the rhetorical opportunism to which Seneca was always prone, but the ease with which Romans adopted the language of courtly panegyric is notable as early as the time of Augustus. However, there was something to be said for an appeal to the more generous enthusiasms of Nero's nature and this could be done by portraying his vast powers and deploying various arguments encouraging him voluntarily to limit their use.

Seneca puts the following sentiments into Nero's mind:

> Have I of all men found favour with Heaven and been chosen to serve on earth as representative of the gods? I am the arbiter of life and death for the nations; it rests in my power what each man's lot and state will be; by my lips Fortune proclaims what gift she would bestow on each human being; from my utterances peoples and cities gather reasons for rejoicing; without my favour and grace no part of the world can prosper. . . . With all things at my disposal, I have been moved neither by anger nor youthful impulse to unjust punishment, nor by the foolhardiness and obstinacy of men which have often wrung patience from even the serenest souls nor yet by that vainglory which employs terror for the display of might. . . . (*De Clementia* I, 1, 2–3.)

The theme was clearly one which appealed to Nero. Seneca had quoted with approval (*De Clementia* II, 1, 1) the emperor's remark made when he was obliged to sign an execution warrant: 'I wish I had never learnt to write.' Suetonius says, no doubt with reference to Nero's early years (*Nero*, 10) that 'he never omitted an opportunity of displaying his generosity, clemency and affability'.

4

Co-operation between Emperor and Senate, 54–62

GOVERNMENT according to the precepts of Augustus meant in practice government which respected as far as possible the pretensions of the Senate, and for some eight years this was what was provided under the influence of Seneca. Conciliatory gestures were numerous. Nero refused the title *Pater Patriae* (Father of his Country), though he then accepted it in 56. He asked the Senate to decree a statue in honour of his father Domitius, and consular insignia for the man who had acted as his guardian on the death of Passienus Crispus, but refused statues in silver and gold for himself. Domitius was honoured in subsequent years, though he did not appear in Nero's official nomenclature. Senatorial flattery in a proposal that the calendar year should begin in December (Nero's birthday month) was rejected. In the face of Agrippina's opposition, the obligation laid by Claudius on quaestors designate to put on gladiatorial shows was removed; it had been a heavy burden on poorer entrants on a senatorial career. Following the practice of former emperors, Nero subsidized members of noble families who had become poor to save them the disgrace of losing senatorial rank, and in 55 excused his colleague in the consulship that year from the annual oath taken by all magistrates to observe the emperor's enactments.

Senatorial opinion ran high on matters of social legislation, particularly that concerning slaves and freedmen, always a source of tension in societies where slave-owning was important. The legislation of Augustus had been conservative, and directed towards preserving the existing social structure, and even Claudius, for all his broad outlook, had not deviated far from traditional Roman attitudes. Thus, the ties binding a freedman to his patron (former owner) had been reaffirmed by two senatorial decrees of Claudian date. In 56 there was a demand that patrons should be able to cancel the freedom of freed slaves who had proved 'undeserving'. The consuls refused to put a formal resolution without consulting the emperor but informed him of the general view of the Senate. Nero's advisers were divided but the final decision was that each case must be judged on its merits. This presumably meant that patrons had to make out a good case, but the door was certainly open for cancellations of freedom.

In 57 there was an addition to a senatorial decree of Augustan date which laid down that when a master had been killed by a slave, all slaves in the house or with the master at the time were liable to the death penalty. In the addition this rule was extended to cover slaves whose manumission was provided for in the master's will. Connected in some way not clear with these rules was an actual event four years later when the city prefect Pedanius Secundus was murdered by a slave. No less than 400 were condemned as accomplices. There was intense sympathy among the poor in the city for the slaves, and rioting outside the Senate House. Nero nevertheless upheld the death penalty and sent in troops to quell the riots, but he rejected a proposal that freedmen who had been in the prefect's house should be expelled from Italy.

Senatorial fears about the slaves and freedmen are notable, and a number of incidents in Rome and Italy show that the possibilities of disturbance or actual revolt were (or were believed to be) never far away. One of the charges against Domitia Lepida in 54 was that she was endangering the peace of Italy by failing to keep her gangs of slaves in Calabria properly under control, while in 64 there was an attempt at escape by gladiators at Praeneste. We may also note Poppaea's claim that it was the slaves and clients of Octavia who constituted the rioters in Rome in 62 (see below, p. 50). Public order in Rome was a serious problem at the best of times. In 55, Nero had withdrawn a cohort from police duties at the games apparently in the hope that they could continue without the oppressive aura of surveillance. The measure had to be revoked the following year because of riots between over-enthusiastic supporters of popular entertainers. Some of these were arrested by a praetor, only to be released by the order of a tribune of the plebs, Antistius Sosianus. This led to an attack in the Senate on the rights of the tribunate. Like the magistrates proper, the tribunes still formally retained their old powers, but they were rarely used. Nevertheless it is curious to see that Antistius' action in defence of citizens experiencing a magistrate's coercive power was in accord with centuries of Republican tradition—as was the Senate's indignant support of the guardians of law and order. As a result, the tribunician power of veto was limited in some way, though not abolished. This restriction was in the interests of the higher magistrates, and also no doubt of the emperor. Since he had tribunician power himself, though not holding the office, it was undesirable that anyone else should exercise its traditionally popular function in defence of the Roman plebs.

The spirit in which justice was administered and in particular the way the emperor took cases in person was important for his reputation. Claudius' enthusiasm for hearing lawsuits himself had been unpopular, so Nero's lack of interest stood him in good stead. In those cases which he was bound to take personally, his practice as described by Suetonius (*Nero*, 15) was unexceptionable: 'In giving judgement, he scarcely ever gave his decisions on the pleas until the day following and then in writing. His practice in hearing the cases was not to allow each side to present its entire case in turn, but to deal with each point in order. When he withdrew to consult his assessors he did not debate the matter openly with them, but silently and in private read over each of their written opinions; he then gave his decisions the way he wanted as if it were the opinion of the majority.' This is all creditable, Suetonius' last sentence being tendentious. To delay judgement for a day was in accordance with the best practice. The next point was undoubtedly of importance in the development of court procedure, since it cut out the long and doubtless often unnecessary speeches of the advocates from which Claudius had suffered; the clarification of each point as it arose was expeditious. As for the method of consultation, the Roman magistrate was in any case not bound by the majority opinion of his assessors. Both Augustus and Claudius had from time to time used the method of written opinions for which there was much to be said, particularly in complex cases. The suggestion that Nero ignored his assessors' opinions perhaps arose from some unpopular decisions for which he could thus be made solely responsible.

The maintenance of order in Italy was one of the responsibilities of the magistrates and Senate. In 58 two delegations came from Puteoli (Pozzuoli) to Rome; the town council accused the mass of the citizens of violence, while the citizens alleged corruption among the magistrates and council. The distinguished lawyer C. Cassius Longinus was sent by the Senate, but asked to be recalled when he had no success in settling the affair. This was said to have been due to his excessive severity—exercised, it may be assumed, in favour of the council; it was Longinus who had been foremost in demanding the extreme penalty in the case of the slaves of Pedanius Secundus. Two brothers of consular rank, the Scribonii, were then given a cohort of the praetorian guard (which shows the emperor working with the Senate) 'and restored harmony by fear and a few executions' (Tacitus, *Annals* XIII, 48). In 59 there were riots between the citizens of Nuceria and Pompeii at a gladiatorial show in the latter town and many were killed. The Nucerians appealed to Nero who properly handed the matter over to the Senate. Pompeii was barred from holding shows for another ten years, and illegal associations in the town were disbanded. Tacitus regarded such violence at the games as typical of Italian towns (though the same sort of thing had happened in Rome a few years before) and this is confirmed for Pompeii by surviving graffiti of this period. There seems to have been no political significance in these disturbances: they were simply examples of a recurring social phenomenon.

If the magistrates and Senate could still exercise some
supervision over Italy, wider aspects of Italian policy
were the concern of the emperor. Augustus had regarded
Italy as the heart of the Empire, and had done a great
deal to repair the ravages of the Civil Wars. He had a
vision of a well-peopled and prosperous land which was
reflected in his social legislation; indeed, concern for the
state of Italy, especially its free population, which was
generally believed to be declining, had been felt by
many statesmen from the second century B.C. and continued to be felt for centuries later. The Augustan laws
are often said to have been a failure, though the evidence
for this is not substantial. His immediate successors seem
to have assumed that they were doing their work and
made no effort to enlarge their scope. Nevertheless, there
were other measures which could be taken to strengthen
urban life in Italy. Claudius, who in general was more
interested in the provinces than in Italy, settled discharged veterans in the old towns of Cumae and Velitrae
(Velletri). Nero's principate, however, shows a concentration of effort on Italian towns which is significant. In
57 the existing *coloniae* of Capua and Nuceria (Nocera)
were strengthened by the addition of veterans, and in 60
Puteoli was raised from municipal to colonial status,
taking the name Colonia Claudia Neronensis. This may
have reference to the continuing importance of the town
as a port of entry to Italy of the Alexandrian corn fleet
and other eastern trade, hardly affected by Rome's new
harbour at Ostia. In the same year veterans from the
praetorian cohorts and rich centurions were added to the
population of Antium and a substantial harbour was
built there; veterans were also added to Tarentum
(Taranto). Pompeii became a colony, probably after an
earthquake in 63, and Tegeanum at some unknown date.

The purpose of the veteran additions is implied by
Tacitus when he writes about Antium and Tarentum:
'They failed to arrest the depopulation, since most of
them [i.e. the new settlers] emigrated to the provinces in
which they had served, leaving no children, since they
were not accustomed to marry and bring up families'

(*Annals* XIV, 27). (Legionaries in service were not permitted to marry.) A declining population was again the problem, but it is notable that most of the attested examples of Nero's concern are seaboard towns. Antium benefited not merely because it was his birthplace but because of the need for better harbours on the inhospitable stretch of coast south of Ostia; Tarentum was an important harbour in the south of Italy which had been eclipsed by Brundisium. The strengthening of Capua and Nuceria and the honouring of Puteoli and Pompeii show an interest in Campanian towns more notable for their commercial and quasi-industrial importance than their agricultural interests. If the population of Italian towns more dependent on agriculture was declining, as it seems to have been at the end of the century, we do not know it. One of the causes of future difficulties is revealed by Tacitus' comment—the preference of discharged legionaries for settlement in the provinces where they had served. Since at this period about half the recruits to the legions stationed in the western and Danubian provinces came from Italy, we must assume a continued drain of active men from this cause, even if not every veteran of Italian origin failed to return to his home town.

The men who composed the imperial government mattered at least as much as the ideas which animated it. The political history of the Republic had largely been that of its ruling class, and since the system of Augustus preserved the hierarchic structure of society, while making the constant renewal from below of the senatorial and equestrian orders an easier and less turbulent process than in the late Republic, analysis of its membership has much to teach us of the inner history of the principate. Struggle for power continued, with family influences, intrigue and bribery all being weapons as before. The favour of the emperor, however, became of decisive importance as a man advanced in his senatorial career; although the semblance of election by his peers lasted up to the praetorship, it is clear that the consulship and the more important governorships were by imperial choice. Historians of the Roman Empire have devoted much attention to changes in the type of person predominant in the administration, and especially to the stages by which one province after another began to be represented in it. The gradual enlargement of the Roman ruling class to include Italians, then men from Spain and southern Gaul followed by other western provinces and finally the east, was a most important historical phenomenon, though it is by no means so certain that each stage was particularly noticeable at the time, and the references to it are few. The absorption of the provincials into the senatorial (and for that matter the equestrian) order was at a modest pace; in the Julio-Claudian era consuls from Italy still outnumber those from the provinces by more than ten to one. This would indicate why Tacitus, who was undoubtedly interested in changes in the governing class and—himself a 'new man'—sensitive about social origins, was not obsessed by them. At a cool look, once the descendants of the Republican nobility had been reduced to a negligible proportion, the Senate of one generation was remarkably similar to that of another. Naturally when provincials reached a position of power they used their influence to support their own friends and relations, strictly in accordance with social custom which laid a heavy obligation on a great man to support anyone who had a claim on him, as the letters of the younger Pliny make so clear.

Thus the fact that two men of provincial origin presided for eight years over a government, the tone of which was thoroughly conservative, was no paradox, nor was the mixture of persons advanced to the consulship or to high commands at all unusual. In 56 Seneca himself held the consulship, as later in the year did L. Duvius Avitus, a native of Burrus' home town Vasio; Avitus went on to command the army of Lower Germany in 58. His predecessor there from 56 was Pompeius Paulinus, who had a double connexion with the two leaders of the régime; he came from Arelate (Arles) in Narbonensis and his sister was married to Seneca. The latter's brother, L. Junius Gallio Annaeanus, likewise received a consulship about this date. These appointments can reasonably be attributed to personal connexions (which is not to say they would not have occurred anyway), and they are not many. Perhaps L. Pedanius Secundus of Barcino (Barcelona) who had been consul in 53 and was made city prefect apparently in 56, and another Spaniard M. Manlius Vopiscus who was consul about 60 may be added to the list. Otherwise no distinguishable pattern can be observed in the consulships, except those held by colleagues of Nero. The emperor's influence being paramount in the choice of consuls, *a fortiori* he was particularly concerned about those whom he would honour by holding the consulship with them. It is notable that apart from his consulship in the final crisis of 68, his consulships were held with men of noble families, three of Republican origin: in 55 L. Antistius Vetus, in 57 L. Calpurnius Piso, in 58 the impoverished M. Valerius Messalla Corvinus and in 60 Cossus Cornelius Lentulus. We may also note the consulship in 55 of the equally noble Cn. Cornelius Lentulus Gaetulicus, son of a conspirator against Gaius. Claudius had shared two out of his four consulships after becoming emperor with his adviser L. Vitellius, but none of Nero's colleagues is recorded as particularly influential. We may therefore conclude that whereas in the first instance Seneca and Burrus were concerned to advance their own connexions, there was also a deliberate attempt to conciliate the element in the Senate most likely to harbour subversive memories of the Republican tradition. Lastly, it may be noted that Thrasea Paetus was consul with Avitus in 56. In spite of the fame gained by Thrasea as an opponent and victim of Nero later in his principate, there is no reason to doubt that he was in sympathy with the tendencies of Seneca's régime, and was in turn useful to it as a notable of Patavium (Padua), one of the richest towns of Italy, and as a man of influence in the Senate.

In 58, when Nero was consul for the third time, the Senate offered him a perpetual consulship—not, it seems, just consular power, but the office itself each year. The significance of the offer and its rejection is obscure.

The offer has been considered an attempt to induce Nero to remain favourable to the Senate by a continuous holding of the supreme Republican magistracy, and his refusal a blow to the hopes of traditionalists. In fact, however, the good relations between the emperor and the Senate continued for several more years, and we have no indication at all of a change in this respect dating from 58. On the contrary, it is the refusal of the offer by Nero which could be described as 'Republican', or rather Augustan, as it was precisely Augustus who, after some years of experiment, found repeated consulships politically disadvantageous—though the Roman proletariat wanted him to continue to hold the office. The offer to Nero was therefore no more than a further example of the Senate's propensity to give the emperor superfluous honours. Tacitus in fact listed it with excessive demonstrations of joy at a victory of Corbulo in Armenia.

The record of senatorial and other governmental measures that can be dated comes almost to an end in 62, the year in which Burrus died and Seneca withdrew from public life. The reasons for the lack of information after this point are obscure (see below, p. 136) but even after 62 there was no immediate breach with the Senate, though the conduct of public business was carried on in a different manner and other advisers were influential. Down to 62, the policy of working in harmony with the Senate had been scrupulously followed. There had been no private, or for that matter public, trials in which members of the senatorial and equestrian orders were victimized; the influence of the emperor's household on affairs had been limited, at any rate after the dismissal of Pallas in 55; the government had shown itself excessively deferential to the prejudices of the upper class, without, however, giving in to its extreme demands in social legislation. It was as a result of the harmony between the Senate and Nero and his advisers that during much of his principate our sources find little to complain of except Nero's crimes and follies in private life; and it was the same harmony that enabled the Senate to overlook them.

5
Nero's Court, 54–62

THE first months of the principate had seemed to crown
the ambitions of Agrippina; she could now hope to
exercise real power in the Empire through her influence
over her son: 'At first Agrippina managed for him all
the business of the Empire . . . she received embassies
and sent letters to various communities, governors and
kings' (Dio, LXI, 3). While this may be generalizing
from particular instances, the Senate was certainly called
to meet in the palace so that Agrippina could listen to
the proceedings from behind a screen, though this did
not prevent it from occasionally acting against her
wishes. It was only with difficulty that Seneca prevented
Agrippina from joining the emperor on his tribunal
when he was receiving ambassadors from Armenia,
which would have been considered humiliating. She
obtained various marks of honour in Rome, though the
only ones specified, besides the inevitable bodyguard,
were the grant of two lictors as attendants, something
Tiberius had refused for his mother Livia, and the
priesthood of the deified Claudius. Without Nero's
knowledge, she procured the death of M. Junius Silanus,
proconsul of Asia in 54, the brother of L. Silanus whom
she had destroyed in 49, and a descendant of Augustus.
He could thus be considered a possible rival; he was at
least a man of senior position, though temperamentally
unsuitable—Gaius had called him 'a golden sheep'. The
death of Narcissus, foremost champion of Britannicus,
followed soon after.

Nevertheless, within a year her power had been
broken by Seneca and Burrus, both of whom owed their
positions to her influence. This was bound to happen.
Amicitia—political alliance among the powerful—was
an emotional and evocative word in Roman public life,
but its effects have sometimes been exaggerated by

43

modern historians. Manifest breaches and quiet evasions of *amicitia* were as common in the Roman as in any other political system. In the case of Seneca and Burrus and Agrippina there could in any case be no real *amicitia*; open political participation by a woman was absolutely excluded, and they need show no loyalty. Their tactics were simple if inglorious; to allow, if not to encourage, the young ruler's addiction to *la dolce vita*, the object being to reduce his interest in the government to the minimum required by the necessities of formal business. Agrippina, on the other hand, was urging him to ceaseless activity and always demanding an account of his actions. In this she was assisted by the efficient Pallas, but her task was hopeless because of Nero's personality and her own exclusion from all direct participation in the making of decisions. The process is seen on the coinage of 54 and 55. In the earliest imperial issues of the new principate, Agrippina appears equal, if not actually superior to Nero; her portrait faces him from the right and his title is relegated to the reverse side of the coin. In issues of 55, however, her portrait is soon subordinated and her title put on the reverse. Many local issues in the east, for example those of Antioch, Alexandria and Nicaea, show her portrait at first, but it disappears after 55.

The beginning of Nero's emancipation from his mother began with his love for a freedwoman, Acte. It was said that he wanted to marry her and that men of consular rank would swear that she was of free, even royal birth; if the story is true, Nero must have given up the idea when faced with the difficulties involved in the divorce of Octavia (see p. 50). Agrippina reacted furiously, not on the grounds of morality, which naturally was not an issue, but because she saw her influence on Nero waning. Nero was equally temperamental; according to Suetonius (*Nero*, 34), 'he was so resentful at his mother's strict enquiries into, and reprimands for, all that he said and did that he exposed her to dislike by threatening to abdicate and go to live in Rhodes.' He then dismissed Pallas, which provoked a fresh crisis;

Agrippina's temper was so violent that she began to threaten Nero with hints about Britannicus.

So at any rate Tacitus alleges, though later he attributed solid arguments to Agrippina to the effect that if Nero were replaced she too would inevitably be killed. Nevertheless, the existence of a faction still supporting Britannicus is probable. It is in this connexion that we may read the extraordinary satire by Seneca generally called *Apocolocyntosis Divi Claudi* (*Claudius turned into a pumpkin*), though much about it remains obscure. The satire was written and presumably circulated in Seneca's circle in Rome shortly after the death of Claudius. Its main object was, it seems, to degrade Claudius and his deification. It has sometimes been found difficult to associate its tone, in places coarsely humorous, with the other works of the philosopher, but there was a tradition of violent and vulgar language in Roman political satire. There was no question of a serious attack on deification as such (which would have involved discrediting Augustus) though no doubt to sensible Romans of the educated class the whole subject was laughable. In the *Apocolocyntosis*, amidst the general mockery of Claudius and his many deficiencies, an important passage is one in which Augustus is made to condemn Claudius' execution of a number of members of the Julian family. Claudius was not a Julian and the implication is that he was in effect an intruder in the imperial office. It thus appears that the deification of Claudius, although it had seemed necessary at the time, was also enhancing the position of Britannicus in some quarters. There may have been many to whom the succession, for the first time, of a son born to the previous emperor was desirable. Shortly before his fourteenth birthday in February 55, the boy died, officially from an epileptic seizure, but it was generally agreed he had been poisoned. Public opinion pardoned the removal of Britannicus on the grounds that the supreme power was indivisible. There were remarkable similarities with the removal of possible rivals on the accession of both Tiberius and Gaius; in the former case Agrippa

45

Postumus had been killed, in the latter, Tiberius Gemellus. Agrippina continued to make mischief by trying to influence officers of the praetorian guard and members of the nobility till finally she was deprived of her bodyguard and left the palace to live in the house of Antonia.

This was as far as matters went. When in the same year Junia Silana accused her of plotting with Rubellius Plautus, another descendant of Augustus, though by blood only from Tiberius, her rebuttal was so formidable that her accusers were punished and some of her friends given important appointments; among these were Faenius Rufus who became prefect of the corn supply and Tiberius Claudius Balbillus, a wealthy Alexandrian, prefect of Egypt. Seneca and Burrus were no doubt content so long as Agrippina refrained from any effort to interfere further in the government. An accusation that Burrus and the retired Pallas were conspiring to supplant Nero by Faustus Cornelius Sulla Felix, descendant of the dictator Sulla, and husband of Claudius' elder daughter Antonia, was rejected out of hand; Burrus himself, though accused, was one of the judges. It was only later that Plautus and Sulla were felt to be a danger.

The murder of Agrippina in 59 occupies an important place in the court history of the period. Not only was it told at length in all the sources but it remained in popular memory as the distinguishing mark of Nero's principate. It was Nero the matricide who was remembered with awe and horror in the humble Jewish and Christian circles in the east in which the so-called Sibylline oracles—a form of eschatological literature—were read. Inevitably Tacitus devoted some of his most powerful passages to it, and indeed treated it at excessive length. However, he failed to indicate any major effect on public opinion, and merely showed that it removed a restraint on Nero's actions. Perhaps, indeed, its immediate effects on Nero's standing were inconsiderable; good relations with the Senate continued for years and there were no popular demonstrations such as occurred at the divorce of Octavia three years later. For Tacitus, the crime seems almost to exist in a vacuum; perhaps it summed up all the crimes committed by Julio-Claudian emperors against members of their own families.

In the question of motive, Tacitus was undoubtedly wrong. He stated that Nero was incited by his mistress Poppaea Sabina, who saw in Agrippina the chief obstacle to Nero's divorce of Octavia. Yet the divorce and marriage to Poppaea did not take place till 62, at which point Tacitus gives other reasons for Nero's unwillingness to divorce Octavia, namely fear of Rubellius Plautus and Faustus Sulla. Other writers, more convincingly, portray Burrus as a particularly firm opponent of the divorce, which did not take place till after his death. As for Poppaea, the sources are in even greater confusion about the origin and progress of her affair with Nero; no less than five different versions (Tacitus providing two) have been identified. There is much to be said for the view that she did not attract Nero's interest till 62 and that the main tradition put the affair earlier in order to associate it with the murder of Agrippina. Thus the matricide remains inexplicable except in terms of a desperate act of Nero to liberate himself from the psychological domination of his mother and enjoy, as we read his friends advised, the fruits of autocratic power. The stories, common to all the sources, that he committed incest with his mother, that he had a mistress who closely resembled her, and reports of bisexual tendencies (and even the fact that his two wives after Octavia were both, it seems, older than himself)—whatever amount of truth there is in them—at least indicate a relationship with Agrippina of a most uneasy kind. There is no hint that she was still engaged in intrigues. Nero, it would seem, had been spoiled by her dominating personality and was unable to reconcile himself to the tensions created by her disapproval. Tacitus indeed ends with this view. Having preceded his account of the crime with the allegations against Poppaea, he follows it by describing Nero as plunging into various excesses from which respect for his mother

47

had previously restrained him—specifically, appearances as a charioteer and, a year later, the institution of the Juvenalia, where he could display his theatrical talents.

The agent of the plot was Anicetus, prefect of the fleet at Misenum and a former teacher of Nero. A ship was built which could be made to fall apart, and Agrippina invited to sail on it in the Bay of Baiae, the whole affair to look like an accident. The attempt failed and Agrippina swam to the shore; thinking that her only hope was to pretend ignorance, she sent a freedman to Nero, who was also at Baiae, saying that she had had a fortunate escape from shipwreck. Nero was panic-stricken and summoned Seneca and Burrus; 'it is uncertain whether they knew of the plot beforehand or not' says Tacitus (*Annals* XIV, 6–7), presumably having different versions before him; Dio alleges that Seneca prompted Nero to the crime. In view of their successful exclusion of Agrippina three years before, this seems very dubious. They now in effect had to decide between the emperor and his mother, and inevitably chose the former. Burrus said that he could not rely on the praetorians to kill Agrippina, as they were loyal to the whole imperial house, so Anicetus carried the murder through with officers of the fleet. The official version was that Agrippina's freedman had been arrested with a weapon in a plot against Nero, while Agrippina herself had committed suicide from consciousness of her guilt. It was some time, however, before Nero ventured to return to Rome. In a letter to the Senate, written (it was said) by Seneca, the official version was given, besides a general attack on Agrippina for her lust for power and for all the bad aspects of Claudius' principate for which she was now blamed. Senatorial decrees of a complimentary kind were inevitably passed, the only sign of disapproval being that of Thrasea Paetus who walked out of the Senate House in silent protest. There seems no doubt that Nero's responsibility was known in spite of the official version, but Agrippina's own past was not such as to win her any sympathy.

Although Nero had had no qualms about Faustus Sulla and Rubellius Plautus at the beginning of his principate, he later became frightened. In 58 Sulla, a relatively poor man, dull and unenterprising, was ordered to go to live in Massilia (Marseille). In 60 popular superstition held that the appearance of a comet heralded a change of ruler, and the name of Plautus was mentioned. Apart from his descent from Augustus, his personality was approved, no doubt as a contrast to Nero: 'He followed tradition, was austere of bearing and his life was respectable and secluded' (Tacitus, *Annals* XIV, 22). Nero asked him to retire to family estates in the province of Asia for the sake of public order in Rome.

Before the next crisis at court, the divorce of Octavia, came the death of Burrus and the retirement of Seneca. Most attributed the former to poison, and only Tacitus properly suggests a doubt; the evidence put forward to justify the charge was of the most trivial kind. To succeed him as praetorian prefect, Nero appointed two men, thus reverting to the position before Burrus. One was Faenius Rufus who was popular because of his honest management of the corn supply; the other was Ofonius Tigellinus who was the more influential with Nero because, it was said, of his depraved character.

Tacitus says that the death of Burrus broke Seneca's political power, and that he asked Nero's permission to retire because without Burrus he felt in an exposed position. Seneca was now some sixty-five years old, and in view of his lifelong interest in intellectual pursuits and his productions in retirement, there seems little reason to doubt that he had had enough of public life. Tacitus' highly stylized description of his final interview with Nero really tells us little except that the historian clearly felt that Seneca's vast wealth acquired in Nero's service needed some excusing (*Annals* XIV, 52-56). It appears that before his death Seneca had in fact returned much of it to the emperor, perhaps as a contribution to the rebuilding of Rome after the fire of 64. Whether Nero was being more than polite in asking Seneca to stay may be doubted. He was now twenty-five and any inclination which he may once have had to follow the advice of elderly men like Seneca and Burrus must have disappeared. His willingness to retain them so long resulted from a combination of the affability he could always show, his basic lack of interest in government, and Seneca's political talents.

The divorce of Octavia was a serious matter for Nero. Superficially it is surprising that the marriage had lasted so long. Nero had no affection for her, and the fact that she had produced no child was an adequate social and political justification for the divorce (though not required by law). In any case, the frequency of divorce and remarriage in the imperial house and the aristocracy generally was notorious. On the other hand, to divorce the previous emperor's daughter, who was popular as one of the few entirely inoffensive ladies of the imperial family, was politically dangerous. Burrus had persistently opposed it and, when Nero kept raising the point, is said to have replied, 'Well then, give her back her dowry', implying the Empire itself. The divorce was therefore one of the consequences of Burrus' death. Before it took place, Tigellinus worked on Nero's fears to procure the death in exile of Sulla and Plautus; no doubt the removal of the two connexions of the imperial house was felt to be an essential precaution before the divorce.

The marriage to Poppaea took place within twelve days of the divorce of Octavia for barrenness. Octavia was given Burrus' house and Plautus' estates but was soon banished to Campania under military surveillance. There were popular protests in Rome and, it appears, a rumour spread that Octavia was to be recalled. In a demonstration of rejoicing, images of Poppaea were overthrown and those of Octavia set up in their place. This settled the fate of Octavia, even if the recorded tirade of Poppaea to her new husband is mere fiction; such demonstrations were always regarded as a most serious threat. After their suppression it was announced that Octavia had committed adultery with Anicetus, still prefect of the fleet, in an attempt to subvert his loyalty and that he had given testimony to that effect. She was banished to the island of Pandateria and executed on 9 June 62. No further disturbances occurred, and Nero's emancipation from the various restraints of family, advisers and conventional behaviour appeared to have had no lasting effect on his position.

6

Provincial Government

IN some respects the most important feature of the principate of Claudius had been his active interest in the provinces of the Empire. It is important not to exaggerate, however; Claudius was not reversing the Augustan conception of Italy as the mistress of the Empire, nor was he inclined to disregard the privileges of Rome and Italy in an attempt to achieve uniformity and equal status for the provinces. This indeed might be the logical outcome of his attitude towards the extension of the Roman citizenship, the most widely known aspect of his provincial policy, but it is unlikely that Claudius would have seen it in this light. He was taking an active interest in the provinces after a generation of immobility, perhaps even neglect, under Tiberius and Gaius. He gave Roman citizenship more widely than had been done since Augustus, but chiefly in the western provinces, and at this stage only a satire could describe the grants as indiscriminate. Claudius at least tried to insist that Roman citizenship only be given to those who knew Latin, which was reasonable enough. On the other hand there is much evidence that under Claudius there was a lot of bribery by candidates for enfranchisement.

The attitude of Nero's government was different. The extension of Roman citizenship was negligible. A number of individuals received the honour, many of them probably Greeks honoured during Nero's visit in 66, but there were no grants to whole communities anywhere in the Empire, nor did Nero found any colonies outside Italy. Only the tiny province called Alpes Maritimae, on the Mediterranean coast between Italy and Gallia Narbonensis, received Latin rights, which meant that the elected magistrates received full Roman citizenship while the rest of the population obtained important rights at Roman law. The neighbouring province of Alpes Cottiae was formed from a client-kingdom on the death of its king. Both measures were no doubt inevitable as Romanization, already entrenched on the far side of the Alps, penetrated the mountainous regions. There can be little doubt that the contrast with Claudius—whose policy was resumed later by Vespasian—was a concession to the Senate which still thought in terms of Italian exclusiveness; it had strongly opposed Claudius' introduction of Gauls into the Senate. Seneca may have agreed, for all that he was a provincial himself; in the *Apocolocyntosis* he had jeered at Claudius' alleged desire to see almost the entire world Roman citizens. It may also be noted that even in his final years of enthusiasm for the Greeks, Nero did not accelerate the pace at which they received the citizenship as individuals or advanced in the equestrian order. He probably believed, and may well have been correct in so doing, that the token gesture of giving 'freedom' to Greece (see below, p. 117) was more desired by the Greeks than the gift of Roman citizenship to a few wealthy individuals. However, the method by which Roman citizenship was now being most extensively given, that is, by grants to honourably discharged auxiliary soldiers, who probably numbered several thousand each year, continued.

At a much higher social level, the careers of Burrus and Seneca exemplify the advance of men from Gallia Narbonensis and Baetica in the equestrian and senatorial orders and reference has been made (above, p. 40) to others whose promotion may be connected with the influence of these two. It was a question of how far a province had advanced from Celtic or Iberian tribalism, or rather of how many men of sufficient wealth, education and Roman manners it had. Within a few years of Nero's death, the elder Pliny wrote of Gallia Narbonensis that it was 'second to no other province in the standing of its men, the worth of its way of life and the extent of its wealth; in short, it is Italy rather than a province' (*Natural History* III, 31). The same was no doubt true of the southern part of Spain, whose leading men seemed to have turned as much to literature as to affairs. We could not deduce from their writings that Seneca, Lucan, Columella and Martial were all Spaniards unless we had external evidence. There could be no objection even by the prejudiced to such men entering the upper class, yet perhaps provincial senators came on too quickly with Seneca and his friends; they were not to be so influential again till the principate of Trajan.

Gallia Narbonensis had been a province for seventy years longer than the rest of Gaul, and was much more attractive to Italian immigrants; it had, besides, an area of older civilization based on the Greek colony of Massilia (Marseille). Its economic growth was greatly assisted when the rest of Gaul was conquered by Julius Caesar. Southern Spain and its Mediterranean coasts had likewise long been open to immigrants, and its mineral wealth in gold, silver, lead and tin was being extensively exploited in Nero's time.

The west and north of Spain were much less influenced by immigration, but these parts were notable recruiting grounds for auxiliaries and Romanization spread rapidly enough for Latin rights to be given to all of Spain shortly after Nero's death. The contrast between the south and north of Gaul was more marked. It is true that Claudius admitted into the Senate notables from the three northern provinces of Gaul, Belgica, Lugdunensis and Aquitania. But whether because after experience the Gallic aristocracy disliked Roman political life, or because they proved unsuitable owing to the essentially non-urban character of their society, relatively few Gauls from the northern provinces entered the Senate. The social structure of Gaul with its extremely wealthy land-owners dominating a large peasant population remained, though a number of new towns took the place of the old Celtic *oppida* and commercial life based on the easy communications provided by the great rivers grew rapidly in the first century. Josephus, writing under Vespasian, makes Herod Agrippa say of Gaul that 'it possesses, as it were, the springs of prosperity in its own

soil, and floods almost the entire world with its products'
(*Jewish War* II, 372). In spite of this, and the influence
of Roman education in such centres as Autun, tribal
feeling remained strong, as the events of 68–70 showed.
Druidism was suppressed with difficulty; human sacrifices had been prohibited by Caesar or Augustus, but
Tiberius and Claudius issued edicts against the cult itself, which survived in decayed form. The wealth of
some of the tribes was attested under Nero, when Autun
employed a Greek sculptor Zenodorus to build a colossal
statue of Mercury which cost forty million sesterces and
was not exceeded in size by Nero's statue at Rome by
the same man.

Urbanization in the Rhineland was slow, and connected chiefly with the forts. The single colonial foundation was Colonia Claudia Augusta Ara Agrippinensium
(Cologne) founded in 51 in honour of Agrippina. Nevertheless, trade with the German tribes was extensive.
Most of it was by routes leading eastwards from the
Rhine from Vetera (Xanten) and Moguntiacum (Mainz),
the rest going north from points on the Danube. The
trade is chiefly identified by Roman coins and material
objects such as silver, pottery and glassware, primarily
from Italy and Gaul, which have been discovered as far
afield as Poland, the Ukraine and Scandinavia. Along
the Rhine (though not, it appears, the upper Danube)
the crossing of the river was under strict control, but
trade continued to grow. What the Romans imported
in return has left little trace; it must be the case that
slaves were included as well as livestock. We know of a
Roman knight in Nero's time travelling from the
Danube to the Baltic and returning with a huge
quantity of amber, a highly prized luxury. Yet the trade
had little effect on the Germans. They used the coins
as personal hoards, or to buy from Roman traders, but
did not develop a money economy. They preferred some
issues of coins to others and were affected by Nero's
depreciation of the denarius. All that the *Pax Romana*
brought to Gaul and the left bank of the Rhine—roads,
towns, larger buildings, higher technical accomplishments

and a general if modest increase in living standards —remained strange to the tribes outside the Empire except as an object of wonder or envy. It is along the Rhine and the Danube that we see most clearly that the success of the Roman Empire was the success not of a superior technology or ideology but of a superior organization.

The evolution of a province was a slow process as can be seen in the case of Africa. Stability had reigned there, as in most of the Empire, since the victory of Julius Caesar, except for a revolt under Tiberius in areas near the desert frontier, and in Mauretania when it was made a province in 40–42. Yet one legion (III Augusta) and its auxiliaries sufficed for the whole area between Cyrenaica and the Atlantic and between the Mediterranean and the desert. The only military problem came from nomads who resented restriction on their movements, and raiders from the mountainous regions, never fully controlled. Yet after nearly a century the African provinces, even the proconsular province which corresponded to most of modern Tunisia and was by far the most evolved, were not ready for massive grants of Roman citizenship. Neo-Punic (a late form of Phoenician) was still spoken in many of the towns. We know little of the stages of urban growth, but it must have been proceeding silently throughout the Julio-Claudian era to make the vitality of the second century in Africa possible. The characteristic of the proconsular province was the very large number of towns both native and Roman, the latter formed from the substantial veteran and proletarian immigration under Caesar and Augustus. This density precluded the development of many vast estates, and medium-sized farms seem to have been the rule. It is not surprising that the first African consul (under the Flavians) came from Cirta (Constantine) in Numidia where settlement was less dense and estates larger.

There were indeed some large estates in Africa; the elder Pliny has the statement, 'To tell the truth, the *latifundia* have ruined Italy and are on the way to ruining the provinces; six landowners possessed half Africa when Nero killed them' (*Natural History* XVIII, 35). *Latifundia* were vast estates worked directly by slave labour, and generally owned by absentee landlords. Their effect on Italian society, especially in the south, had been felt from the second century B.C. and to deplore them was a commonplace. It is not clear, however, over how wide an area they predominated. An inscription from Ain el-Djemila in western Tunisia may refer to an imperial estate formed from Nero's confiscations— it refers to *saltus* (estates) named Neronianus, Lamianus, Domitianus and Blandianus. The area they covered is very far from being 'half Africa', and Pliny's statement was merely rhetorical. He was also incorrect in his forebodings. The chief obstacle to the *latifundia* in Africa was the density and vitality of the towns, but it is possible that there were not enough slaves from the start. At any rate within a short time we find on the imperial estates and on neighbouring private estates tenancies on a share-cropping basis, which survived in the area for centuries. There can be no doubt that the agricultural production of Africa rose throughout this period, and a vast amount was exported to Rome. It was said (under Vespasian) that whereas the contribution of Egypt to Rome's corn supply sufficed for four months, that of the African provinces sufficed for eight. This is not impossible, Africa's importance to Rome no doubt increased with Claudius' new harbour at Ostia through which all African products came. In 68 the rebel Clodius Macer was able to threaten famine at Rome by withholding corn supplies from Africa.

In Syria and Asia Minor, the activity of Nero's government can hardly be traced, though the long war in Armenia and the Parthian threat to Syria, which brought concentrations of legions and mobilization of local levies, must have had some effect. Nero's philhellenic interests were in practice confined to artistic matters, and though he intended to visit Alexandria and perhaps to take part in a campaign in the Caucasus, in fact he only visited Greece (see below, p. 116). Furthermore, it may be noted that no more Greeks were influential in the administration under Nero than under Claudius, and some of them, such as Ti. Claudius Balbillus and Ti. Julius Alexander, were completing careers begun earlier. Only a dozen Roman knights (and no senators) of Greek origin are known from the two principates. This was not due to Roman exclusiveness; Nero would no doubt have approved candidates from the Greek world, and, whatever prejudice might say, their utility in financial administration in the Greek provinces was obvious. Many possessed the fortune needed to enter the equestrian order, though the influence of friends in Rome was probably more difficult to acquire. The real reason was a lack of interest on their part. Even Roman citizenship, useful to those engaged in commerce and perhaps increasingly as a mark of status, was acquired by only a small minority. Again, most equestrian posts were military, and there was no tradition in the east to fit men for this sort of service. It is also significant that those known to us do not come from the great cities like Ephesus, Miletus, Laodicea or Syrian Antioch. They come from small towns, or are rootless. Thus Gessius Florus, procurator of Judaea 64–66, came from Clazomenae, an old but small place; Antonius Felix, procurator of Judaea 52–60, was a freedman and brother of Pallas; C. Caecina Tuscus, prefect of Egypt 62–66, was the son of a freedwoman. The leading men of the cities of Greek Asia and Syria, still more those of Greece itself, still preferred the traditional life of a Greek magnate within the city and could satisfy their ambitions there. The epigraphic evidence which indicates the vitality of city life in the east is complemented by the narrative in *Acts* of Paul's journeys which took him to many cities under Claudius and Nero. At the end of the century Plutarch still expressed the ideals of the city aristocracy in the traditional way, though he recognized the limitations imposed by Roman rule. Two men from Alexandria, the largest city in the east, Ti. Claudius Balbillus, prefect of Egypt 55–59, and Ti. Julius Alexander, prefect of Egypt 66–70, do not disprove the argument; Alexandria was not permitted to have a regular civic organization in which its magnates could function, and Alexander, as a Hellenized Jew, would have had no firm position in either the Greek or the Jewish community.

A number of trials of provincial governors for various offences were held between 54 and 61, more than in equivalent periods under other emperors of which we have detailed knowledge. Although provincials were better protected against misgovernment under the principate than in the Republic, the improvement was in the diminution of the temptations of governors and a somewhat more effective enforcement of the laws rather than in the laws themselves. There was no diminution of the governors' powers of justice and execution. All proconsuls and imperial legates had full *imperium* and governors of equestrian rank were specifically granted equivalent powers. Naturally a conscientious emperor would not wish his reputation to be tarnished by the activities of an extortionate governor or procurator, but provincials might be reluctant to pursue a man who had been appointed by the emperor. Certainly there seem to be few prosecutions of imperial procurators compared with the frequent complaints about them. In the Republic, laws against extortion and corruption had been numerous and severe; the problem was their enforcement. Under the principate, the Senate seems to have tried all cases, including those of equestrian governors till about 60, and can be accused of leniency.

Twelve prosecutions in this period are recorded, of which six were successful. In 56 Vipsanius Laenas, procuratorial governor of Sardinia, was convicted of extortion; in 57 Cossutianus Capito, *legatus* of Cilicia, fell to a determined prosecution, which included Thrasea Paetus, and was expelled from the Senate (to be reinstated at a later date through the influence of his father-in-law Tigellinus); and in 60 Vibius Secundus was exiled from Italy on charges of extortion in Mauretania, saved from severer punishment by the influence of his brother Vibius Crispus. These three were imperial appointments. Convicted governors of senatorial provinces were:

Pedius Blaesus (Cyrene) in 59 for accepting bribes and petitions to falsify the rolls of those liable to recruitment —provincial levies were a potent cause of discontent; Tarquitius Priscus (Bithynia) in 61 and an unknown Scaevinus. Those acquitted were Cestius Proculus (Crete) in 56, Eprius Marcellus (Lycia) in 57, Sulpicius Camerinus and Pompeius Silvanus (Africa) in 58, Acilius Strabo (Crete) in 59 and the procurator Celer (Asia) in 58. Eprius Marcellus, later a notable prosecutor in treason trials, was said to have been so effective in his intrigues that some of his accusers were punished, by implication, unjustly. The two proconsuls owed their acquittal to Nero, who presumably voted for it in the Senate, with a suggestion of undue influence in the case of Silvanus. Acilius Strabo had had a special commission from Claudius to adjudicate on disputes concerning the ownership of old royal land, now strictly belonging to the Roman state, which had been occupied by private persons. He had decided against the latter. The Senate referred the case to the emperor saying they did not know Strabo's instructions—in fact he was still working in the province at the beginning of Nero's reign. Nero upheld his decisions but as an act of grace legalized the occupation by private persons, presumably on the grounds of length of occupation. Nero is said to have delayed the trial of Celer till his agent died because of his part in the execution of Silanus, though since this was inspired by Agrippina the charge seems unlikely. Finally, there was a case concerning Italy about which Tacitus wrote (*Annals* XIII, 30): 'Clodius Quirinalis, commander of the fleet at Ravenna, who had inflicted his savagery and debauchery on Italy as if it were the most despised of territories, poisoned himself to forestall condemnation.'

There is little difference between imperial and senatorial provinces as regards effective justice in the above list, and Nero is blamed only once. It has been argued that most prosecutions at this period and in other well documented periods of first and second century history came from Greek-speaking provinces which knew their rights and on the whole were richer and able to take steps to protect themselves. Yet Sardinia and Mauretania were not wealthy, though they both had many Roman citizens who would know how to set about things, and the same is true of Cyrene. The imperial government knew well enough the ways of perverting justice, and not only in the Senate House itself. In 58 'Nero ordered that no provincial governor should put on any gladiatorial or wild beast show or any other amusement in his province. Previously, such liberality had been as oppressive to the provincials as actual extortion, since the governors thereby defended their illegalities by winning supporters' (Tacitus, *Annals* XIII, 31). In any event, wealthy provincials could protect themselves—though they might easily be oppressive to the poor of their own communities. In 62 a certain Cretan, Claudius Timarchus, presumably a Roman citizen, was prosecuted 'on the charges generally brought against powerful provincials, who, puffed up with excessive wealth, oppress their inferiors' (Tacitus, *Annals* XV, 20). He was also alleged to have remarked that it depended on him whether or not a governor of Crete should receive a vote of thanks from the provincial assembly. Thrasea Paetus spoke in fierce terms against this practice, arguing among other things that whereas once the fate of whole nations had depended on the verdict of an individual Roman, governors now curried favour with provincials to obtain congratulatory addresses. In spite of the nostalgic reference to the more aggressive days of Roman imperialism, there was obviously a good case for curbing the dependence of governors on the good will of provincial magnates. As a result of general approval of Thrasea's sentiments, Nero agreed to a senatorial decree which forbade votes of thanks from provincial assemblies to governors. This in fact was an extension of an Augustan rule against the grant of honours to a provincial governor till at least sixty days after his retirement.

Tacitus' record of prosecutions of governors ends in 61, just as his record of specific governmental measures ends the next year. Whether or not later governors merited prosecution we do not know—though in view of the exigencies of Nero's last years prosecutions would have had little chance of success. While the prosecutions reveal what opportunities for corruption and extortion still existed, they also indicate that in the view of the provincials the government had a real interest in the good conduct of provincial affairs and that a proper hearing of complaints was to be expected. There is no reason to doubt that although the régime of Seneca lacked the interest which Claudius had had in such matters as the extension of Roman citizenship, it was fully determined to maintain what had been the ideal of Roman government in the provinces since the time of Augustus. The maintenance of strict justice for provincials was, after all, fully in line with the paternalistic ideas of the *De Clementia.*

7

The Imperial Finances

IN the Roman Empire, economic changes were so slow, and are so little known in detail, that they can generally be measured only by centuries or half centuries rather than by individual principates. For Nero's time, we can say little more than that the process whereby the productive forces of some of the provinces came to rival and then to exceed those of Rome and Italy was just beginning. The external trade of the Empire was continuing on the line of development begun under Augustus, though some interesting details are known. Nero's fiscal policy is better attested, and seems to fall into two periods, the first one of general prudence, the second one in which a combination of factors led to a deterioration.

It is not unreasonable to associate the first period with the financial talents of Seneca and the experience of Burrus. The administration of the imperial finances is an obscure subject and the controversies about it cannot even be outlined here. Formally speaking, public revenues and expenditures were the responsibility of the *Aerarium Saturni* (Treasury of Saturn), a survival from the Republic and under the authority of the Senate. But in practice the emperors, beginning with Augustus, not only acquired a more or less strictly defined control over the Treasury but established a parallel financial structure of their own (the *Fiscus*), and although Augustus published imperial accounts this practice was subsequently discontinued. The expenditure of the emperor included the cost of the army and the fleet, the corn and money distributions to the citizens, and public building, not to mention his own household. The revenues of the imperial provinces were presumably allotted to him to set against this expenditure, but can never have sufficed in spite of the revenues drawn from Egypt. Yet we frequently hear of grants from the emperor to the Treasury rather than the other way round. This was possible because of the continuing and rapid growth of the wealth of the emperor whose private fortune played an increasingly important part in public finance. Since there were no public accounts, it is not really surprising that our sources are generally unable to distinguish between what the emperor paid from his own and what he paid from imperial revenues. Additions to the imperial fortune (which being in land produced a substantial income) came primarily from legacies, since social custom dictated that the rich include bequests to Caesar in their wills. It also benefited from intestacies and the property of condemned criminals, notoriously those condemned for treason, in most cases wealthy senators and knights.

Nero replaced the quaestors of the Treasury by two prefects chosen from ex-praetors. This retained the practice of imperial appointment to a position nominally within the Senate's competence but brought in men of greater experience and seniority. It is probable that inefficiency in the years before this change led Nero to support the Treasury with forty million sesterces to maintain public confidence. An indication of the way in which the administration of the emperor's private fortune had become inextricably bound up with public finance is indicated by the circumstances of the retirement of Pallas in 55; he secured assurances that he would not be called to answer for any past action and that his account with the Treasury should be deemed to be in balance. This indicates that he had financial responsibilities other than those for which he was responsible solely to the emperor, and in any case he alone would know all the details. Nero remarked in this connexion: 'He is going to swear himself out of office', the point of the joke being that his freedman was effectively acting like a magistrate of the Roman people.

The most famous venture of Nero into financial matters occurred in 58 when he had the idea—though he did not go so far as to propose it formally—of abolishing all indirect taxes (*vectigalia*) in the Empire. The most important of these were the custom duties (*portoria*) levied at the imperial frontiers, at the boundaries of financial districts within the Empire, and often at individual harbours. It is erroneous to see in this a vision of the economic advantages of free trade which, contrary to a common assumption, never existed in the Roman Empire. This was beyond the economic thinking of antiquity. The description by Tacitus of the origin of the idea and its final consequences makes it quite clear that it arose from the continuing complaints about the private tax-gatherers (*publicani*) who collected the indirect taxes. The hatred aroused by these persons in earlier Roman history is notorious, and although their sphere of activity was much reduced by Augustus, their opportunities for extortion were still considerable. Tacitus says (*Annals* XIII, 50) that Nero was persuaded to drop the scheme on the grounds that the Empire would collapse if the revenues which sustained it were diminished, since abolition of indirect taxes would only lead to a demand for the abolition of direct taxes. This extraordinary argument looks characteristically Tacitean; presumably it was put that direct taxes (land- and poll-tax) would have to be increased to compensate for the loss of the *vectigalia*, and this would be even more unpopular than the activities of the *publicani* since more people would be affected. The proposal seems to be one of the superficially well-meaning but ill-considered ideas characteristic of Nero, but which he was prepared to drop on advice. In the event, he was content to issue an edict ordering the publication of regulations governing each tax, hitherto confidential. Claims to arrears were to lapse after a year and governors were to give priority to cases against *publicani*. Other regulations were included, but almost all were soon evaded.

The prudence of his advisers was justified. In 62 he set up a powerful commission of three men of consular rank to supervise at least the indirect taxes—presumably still closer control of the *publicani* must have been envisaged; it is possible that the entire revenue of the Treasury was to be looked at. Nero criticized previous emperors for undertaking excessive expenditure in advance of income and said that he was subsidizing the state to the amount of sixty million sesterces a year. This figure is not impossible. Augustus claimed to have given the state 2,400 million sesterces, which if averaged over the years 27 B.C. to 14 produces an annual figure similar to Nero's. Such commissions had been set up by Augustus and Claudius, and were later used by Vespasian and Nerva to deal with important financial problems. The difficulties in 62 were probably caused by the wars in Armenia and Britain.

It is not impossible that the change in the monetary system of the Empire in 64 was the result of the advice of Nero's commission. Nero's coinage as a whole has a number of remarkable features. The coins are some of the finest in design and execution ever produced in Rome. Particularly noteworthy is the series of portraits of the emperor himself, uncompromising in their realism. There can be no doubt that this was due to the art-loving emperor. We have no evidence for the precise mode by which dies were approved or rejected, but it must be presumed that at some stage the emperor in person was concerned. It was at this point that the interest of a man who had pronounced views on the subject would be felt.

Politically, a novel feature was the appearance of the formula *EX S.C.* ('in accordance with a decree of the Senate') on gold and silver coins. Previously, references to the Senate had only appeared on the copper coinage of the Empire and it has often been said that the emperor was responsible for the gold and silver coinage, the Senate for the copper. In fact, a 'senatorial coinage' never existed under the Empire. It was the emperor who controlled the coinage of all sorts, both for economic reasons and because it was such an important method of proclaiming the aspirations and claims of the government. Gold and silver were issued from mints directly under his control, copper coinage through the agency of the Senate—hence the reference on the coins. The appearance of a reference to the Senate on the coinage in precious metals from which it had rigorously been excluded under earlier emperors is completely in line with a policy of working with and through the Senate. It began in combination with an oak-wreath, representing the 'civic crown', perhaps really decreed by the Senate as an honour to Nero and continued on the coins till the reform of 64 when it disappeared—for ever. The brief power of Agrippina is faithfully mirrored on the coinage (see above, p. 44) but after her eclipse and till 64 the coin types fit the theme of senatorial co-operation. The portraits always show Nero bareheaded and no effort is made to make his person transcendent in any way. The reverses of the coins are similarly in traditional vein, portraying (in succession to the oak-wreath) Ceres, symbolizing peaceful prosperity, Roma, the capital city, and *Virtus*, the essence of the Roman tradition.

Nero minted no copper coinage till the reform of 64 though there is no clear reason for this. Presumably it was estimated that there was sufficient in circulation, and it is certainly true that the copper coinage was not subject to wastage outside the Empire as was that of precious metal. In 64 two changes occurred. *Aurei* (gold coins) were minted at 45 to the pound of gold as opposed to 42, and *denarii* (silver) at 96 to the pound as opposed to 84. The ratio of gold to silver remained almost the same as before, but the reduction of weight brought a gain to the Treasury, however temporary it might be. At the same time a complete series of coins of small denomination was issued in orichalcum, the units being sestertius (4 asses), dupondius (2 asses), as, semis ($\frac{1}{2}$ as) and quadrans ($\frac{1}{4}$ as). This system was abandoned shortly after for unknown reasons in favour of the old, *viz.* orichalcum for sestertius and dupondius, copper for as and quadrans.

It has often been supposed that there was an incipient shortage of precious metal, especially gold, because of a continued drain from the Empire to the east in payment for luxury imports. The emperor Tiberius complained about the shortage of currency, and the elder Pliny was also concerned. It is certainly true that the bulk of the

Empire's external trade was with Arabia and India. The staple of the Arabian trade was the incense which was an essential requirement of almost all ancient religions. The trade with India was largely in spices, perfumes and precious stones. It had greatly developed during the principate of Augustus and the decisive factor was the discovery, or at any rate the publication of the knowledge, of the way the monsoon could be used to aid navigation. The moralizing instincts of the elder Pliny were offended by the trade; he says that at the funeral of Poppaea the consumption of incense was equivalent to a whole year's supply from Arabia, and that the latter country was the richest in the world because it accumulated gold and silver from Rome (and Parthia) but bought nothing in return. According to Pliny the drain of gold and silver to Arabia and India and beyond amounted to a hundred million sesterces a year, of which a half went to India.

It is certainly true that there was a considerable export of coin from the Empire; many thousands have been discovered in south India. The silver coinage of emperors later than Nero hardly occurs, however, yet trade is known to have continued and even increased. It is likely that one reason was the depreciation of the coinage by Nero, but this did not lead to the rejection in India of his gold coins. It is possible, if Pliny's views were widely held, that the Romans imposed some prohibition on the export of coinage, and that other products of the Empire found a market in India. In any case, Roman fears were perhaps exaggerated; Pliny himself has vivid descriptions of the triumphs of Roman engineering in the gold mines of Spain which produced 20,000 lbs a year (nearly equal in value to his figure for the drain to the east) and records the discovery of a productive new source in Dalmatia which produced 50 lbs a day. In fact, Nero's rate for gold was maintained for over a century, and it was the silver coinage which continued to be depreciated.

In the latter part of Nero's principate, there were serious financial difficulties. These were due to his extravagant projects both public and private which far outstripped imperial revenues. Tacitus, Suetonius and Dio unite in saying that the problem of finance became acute after the fire of Rome in 64 and allege general ruin in the provinces. There can be no reason to doubt the seriousness of the problem in view of the known size of projects such as the *Domus Aurea* (Nero's new palace), the Tiber–Avernus canal and the Corinth canal (see below, p. 133), not to mention the lavish expenditure on the visit to Rome of Tiridates of Armenia in 66. The Roman Empire, it should not be forgotten, lived financially from hand to mouth. The Treasury's reserves of gold were quickly run down by sudden increases in expenditure, and modern techniques of financing deficits by long-term borrowing were unknown. The only alternatives when more revenues were needed were increased taxation or the seizure of the property of the rich, both unpopular and the latter dangerous as well.

Nero is one of a number of emperors who were accused of having men condemned to death for treason when the real motive was to get hold of their wealth— confiscation of property was an additional consequence of conviction for treason. Literary sources refer to such victims in Rome, Africa and Greece, but the truth is impossible to determine. On the other hand, while it is unlikely that the imposition of new taxes would not have been mentioned by our sources, it seems that procurators were given instructions to maximize existing revenues. Nero is said to have told every office-holder 'You know what I need' or 'Let us see to it that no one is left with any property' (Suetonius, *Nero*, 32). When Vindex revolted in 68 one factor in his favour was the unpopularity of the government's fiscal exactions, and in Spain Galba was moved to sympathize with those who were being harried by Nero's procurators. A famous inscription from Egypt, known as the Edict of Tiberius Julius Alexander (Smallwood, 391) and issued in the first weeks of Galba's principate, refers to a number of abuses in the previous years which it was the purpose of the new régime to correct. Allowing for a propagandist element, the edict indicates heavy pressure on the resources of Egypt which of all the Roman provinces can most properly be said to have been exploited. Some ten years of prudent economies by Vespasian were required to restore the financial position of the Empire.

8

Defence of the Empire

THE elder Pliny (*Natural History* VI, 181) wrote that
Nero 'among his other wars, even thought of an Ethio-
pian campaign', which, however, never materialized.
Pliny's references to Nero are generally unfavourable,
and this one is no exception. It implies that Nero's principate saw too much war and that at least one project was
unprofitable. Obviously, a Roman of a traditional cast
of mind was the last to be disturbed by war in itself;
Pliny had himself written a book entitled *Bella Ger-
maniae* covering all the wars that Rome had ever waged
against the Germans down to perhaps 47. But the
Germans had been considered for generations to be dangerous enemies of Rome, very properly the object of
intimidatory as well as of defensive wars. The trouble
with Nero's principate was that two serious revolts, the
British and Jewish, occurred within the Empire and
with considerable loss; the Armenian war dragged on
for nine years with a final compromise achieved by diplomacy rather than by fighting; and projected campaigns
in the directions of the Caucasus and Ethiopia (the
modern Sudan) never took place and in any case were
probably unnecessary. Only the solid maintenance of
the Rhine and Danube frontiers was creditable. The
revolts were probably most offensive to Pliny, whose
Natural History contains some notable, if traditional,
expressions of the benefits to the human race of the *Pax
Romana*. Nero's principate could in this respect, as in
so many others, be contrasted unfavourably with that of
Vespasian.

It was indeed ironic that the most unwarlike ruler of
the century should be faced with a succession of military
problems. An emperor was not expected to go on every
campaign, but Nero never visited his soldiers and seems
to have lacked interest in them altogether. It is not

wisdom after the event which judges this as most serious
for his own position; his predecessor Claudius, almost
as un-military, had been extremely careful to cultivate
the army. Notably, he had himself hailed *imperator* no
less than twenty-seven times, most of which must have
celebrated trifling successes. Nero really had a better
claim, yet took the imperial salutation only twelve times.
Again, the crafty Vespasian, for whom the restoration
and consolidation of the frontiers after the troubles of
68–69 took precedence over all else, and who certainly
had no military ambition beyond this, received twenty
imperial salutations.

In the last analysis, therefore, Nero's personal responsibility seems to have ended with the choice of governors
for the provinces in which there were military forces,
and the approval of measures to back them up if trouble
occurred. As will be seen, the majority of his appointments were adequate from a military point of view,
though the deficiencies of the imperial administration
were otherwise revealed by the outbreaks of revolt. It is
not known to which advisers Nero turned in making his
appointments or in determining strategy, except in one
case. Tacitus discusses the opinions current in Rome
when Nero, at the very beginning of his principate, was
faced with the possibility of a war with Parthia, and says
that there was confidence because Seneca and Burrus
were known as men of great experience (*Annals* XII, 6).
Yet neither was a man with experience of war; Burrus
seems never to have held a military post between his
tribunate and the command of the praetorian guard.

1. BRITAIN AND THE REVOLT OF BOUDICCA

The initial stages of the conquest of Britain had been
relatively easy for the Romans, and within four years of
the invasion in 43 the wealthiest part of the country,
south of a line running roughly from Lincoln to south
Devon, had been overrun or had submitted. Further
advance into more difficult country westwards was

slower, the Silures of south Wales offering particularly stubborn resistance even after the capture in 51 of the chieftain Caratacus who had led them and others since shortly after the invasion. The governor at the time of Nero's accession was Didius Gallus. The appointment in

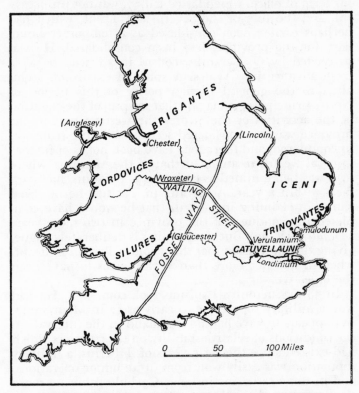

BRITAIN IN THE TIME OF NERO

52 of this elderly politician, who had been consul in 36 and (so far as is known) had had no military experience since his visit to the island in the company of Claudius, may be due to internal politics at Rome and the need of a 'safe' man while Agrippina strengthened her position; it certainly shows no alarm at the military situation. He

repulsed raids by the Silures and their attacks seem to have stopped; elsewhere he made small advances, and was able to maintain in power Cartimandua, pro-Roman queen of the Brigantes, the largest tribe in northern Britain. Tacitus was faintly contemptuous of Didius, but his term of office, which lasted till 57, was not unsuccessful, and the line of the Severn and Trent, which had perhaps earlier been considered as a temporary boundary for the province, had been consolidated. He was succeeded by Q. Veranius, consul in 49, who began a fresh advance into Wales. A spirit of expansion seems alien to the general foreign policy of this period of Nero's principate; it may be that in spite of the cessation of the activities of the Silures the western part of the province was not considered secure while the tribe was unconquered, and there may have been hopes of further mineral wealth to augment that of the Mendips, where lead was being mined as early as 49. Veranius, however, died within a year. According to Tacitus, he betrayed vanity in claiming in his will that he would have completed the conquest of the province in two more years (*Annals* XIV, 29). But the wording is deliberately vague, giving the impression that the whole of Britain is meant, when in fact not more than Wales seems to have been the objective.

In 58 C. Suetonius Paulinus took command. He had won a military reputation as early as 42 in Mauretania, but appears to have had no command in the interval. In the conditions of relative stability on the frontiers which had existed since the early years of Tiberius, a military reputation was easily won from quite minor operations, and in some cases, for instance Corbulo, from no more than efficient discipline. Corbulo and Suetonius were said to be rivals, Suetonius hoping to equal Corbulo's Armenian success. He seems to have been able to turn at once to the subjugation of north Wales, which presupposes good results from Veranius' campaign. The main objective was Anglesey, fertile and populous, an asylum for refugees and a source of help to the rebellious. The two years of campaigning needed to reduce north Wales, including Snowdonia, seem to have been devoid of major incident. No doubt the methodical preparations from the base at Chester and a force of two legions (XIV Gemina and XX Valeria Victrix) with auxilaries proved overwhelming. Even the crossing of the Menai Strait, potentially hazardous, was easily accomplished, though it provided Tacitus with a famous set-piece describing the ranks of the Britons inspired by dishevelled black-robed women and the prayers of the Druids. It was while he was destroying the sacred groves where human sacrifices had been performed that Suetonius heard of the revolt of the Iceni.

In 59 Prasutagus, the client-king of the Iceni, had died. In the hope that his kingdom and family would be fairly treated after his death, he had made the emperor his heir, along with his two daughters. No doubt he was well aware that the continuation of his tribe's client status was improbable, and in fact its incorporation into the province was ordered. But the Romans on the spot treated the tribe as if it was newly conquered territory; Prasutagus' wife Boudicca was flogged and her daughters raped, tribal notables were driven from their lands and royal kinsmen enslaved. Fearing still worse when provincialization was complete, the tribe took up arms, inspiring others who had secretly promised support. Among these the Trinovantes were prominent, as they had suffered from the settlement by Claudius of a colony of veterans at Camulodunum (Colchester) in their territory and from further illegal seizure of land from the native population. Finally, the expenses of the cult of Claudius in the temple erected to him in his own lifetime at Camulodunum were ruining the tribal notables.

Such is Tacitus' account of the causes of the revolt, with the blame laid entirely on the Romans—the staff of the procurator Decianus Catus, the centurions backing him up and the aggressive colonists. Whether it is the whole story is another matter. The brutality of the Roman soldiery was a common theme of Tacitus, especially in the *Histories*, nor has he many good words to say about procurators. The narrative of the revolt is coloured by an intermittent fancy of the historian, that of the Noble Savage and his fight for liberty; the corresponding passage on Boudicca in the *Agricola* is wholly rhetorical on the subject. Nevertheless it must be remarked that the commonplaces of ancient historians often corresponded to reality. The brutality of the peasant soldiers and the rapacity of imperial procurators are well attested in each generation of imperial history. Dio (LXII, 2) has a different version of the causes of the revolt, though the procurator Decianus Catus appears again; he demanded that the grants of money which Claudius had given to the tribal notables should be returned. Another reason was said to be that Seneca, who had lent forty million sesterces to the Britons, recalled it all at once. In view of Seneca's vast wealth, this has been found an attractive theme, although Dio's hostility to Seneca is well known. The silence of Tacitus, who knew well enough the charges of extortionate money-lending that were made against Seneca and who had a keen eye for hypocrisy, is worth more than Dio's accusation.

The Romans had been confident of the loyalty of the tribes. Camulodunum was unwalled, and only a few hundred soldiers were immediately available. The revolt spread beyond East Anglia to the Midlands. Dio's portrait of the warrior queen, Boudicca, tall, red-haired and fierce of aspect, and dressed in tartan tunic and plaid addressing her warriors spear in hand, owes much to convention, but Tacitus confirms her acceptance as leader by all the rebels. The first attack was on Camulodunum. The procurator Decianus, who was at London, was appealed to, but sent only 200 half-armed men. These and the residents could not even build ditches or ramparts. The town was taken and burnt to the ground. On hearing of the rising, the commander of IX Hispana, Q. Petilius Cerealis, later a prominent figure under Vespasian, marched with part of his army from Lincoln, but was met on the way; most of his infantry was destroyed but he escaped with his cavalry. The defeat of the nearest legion deprived the rest of the south-eastern part of the country of any hope and Decianus fled to Gaul.

Suetonius' first concern was for the safety of London, which, although it did not have colonial or municipal status, was the richest town in the province, and the main port of entry. Leaving his infantry to follow he led his cavalry through rebel territory, at the same time ordering II Augusta to join him. This legion, at Gloucester, could have arrived almost as soon as Suetonius' cavalry, but its temporary commander failed to obey the order. Suetonius then decided that London could not be held, as it was unwalled. Only a small part of the population was able to accompany him as he fell back on his infantry. The Britons destroyed the town and followed this with the destruction of Verulamium (St. Albans). Tacitus refused to describe the atrocities committed on the inhabitants, but Dio gives a gruesome account which there is little reason to doubt, whether the Britons were anxious to involve all the rebels in a collective crime to increase their solidarity or (more likely) were driven by the savage streak in Celtic religion. Tacitus states that 70,000 Roman and allied citizens perished; Dio's figure of 80,000 is probably influenced by the number massacred by Mithridates in Asia in 88 B.C. The figures are not impossible; the number of traders who swarmed to newly conquered areas was a feature of Roman expansion, and many of the victims will have been Britons who had not joined the revolt.

Suetonius assembled XIV Gemina and detachments of XX Valeria Victrix with auxiliaries, a force of 10,000 men, all that could be spared if the revolt was not to spread further. Somewhere in the midlands a battle with the main force of the rebels took place and a Roman victory said to have been of classic proportions ensued. Boudicca committed suicide. The resistance of the rebels nevertheless continued though they suffered severely from famine. Suetonius received 2,000 legionaries from the Rhine army, a cavalry contingent of 1,000 men and eight auxiliary cohorts to make up his losses. During the

77

winter the territories of the resisting tribes were harried. However, a new procurator, C. Julius Alpinus Classicianus,[1] a member of a notable family of the Rhineland tribe of the Treviri, urged Nero to replace Suetonius by a less ruthless governor, as otherwise peace was impossible. No doubt his concern was for the diminished revenues of the province. Nero sent one of his freedmen, Polyclitus, to try to settle the differences between the general and procurator and to pacify the tribes. He may have had some success, and his report to Nero minimized the dispute. Suetonius was not recalled till, so it was said, a suitable pretext was found in the loss of some ships, and he was succeeded by Petronius Turpilianus in the second half of 61. Suetonius was not given triumphal *insignia*, but was clearly not disgraced as he had the rare honour of a second consulship in 66.

There was little military activity in Britain during the rest of the principate of Nero. Petronius put an end to the last resistance, which may well have been negligible. He may not have been so unmilitary a figure as Tacitus implies in the words, 'He neither provoked the enemy nor was provoked by them, and called this ignoble activity peace with honour' (*Annals* XIV, 39); he was in charge of the mobilization of forces in Italy in the final crisis of Nero's rule, and was one of the very few men of high rank executed by Galba. In 63 he was succeeded by Trebellius Maximus, who held the command till 69; he had had no previous military command. His administration was conciliatory to the provincials, and involved a no doubt modest start to the re-establishment of urban life.

The conquests of Veranius and Suetonius in Wales were given up as a result of the crisis caused by the revolt of Boudicca, and expansion was only resumed under Vespasian. This may have seemed inglorious to traditionalists but the military position in Britain had improved so much by 67 that Nero was able to withdraw XIV Gemina for his eastern projects. According to Suetonius (*Nero*, 18) 'he even thought of withdraw-

[1] His tombstone (Smallwood, 268) is in the British Museum.

78

ing the army from Britain and only gave up the idea from shame at seeming to detract from his father's glory'. Various dates have been suggested for this proposal but arguments for a date immediately after news of the revolt reached Rome are substantial. The situation reported by Catus Decianus, who would not have minimized its gravity if only to justify his flight, would have included the news that the *colonia* had fallen, that a legion had been defeated and that Suetonius Paulinus and his force were over 200 miles away, cut off from the south-east of Britain. Subsequent news would have been that the general had found the situation so bad that he had had to give up London, his main supply base, and retreat into the interior of the island. A disaster could be feared, comparable to the Pannonian revolt of 6 when Augustus thought of committing suicide, and the loss of three legions in Germany in 9. On this occasion, panic produced one of Nero's hasty and unconsidered ideas, which he was, however, prepared to be argued out of. The appeal by his advisers to the reputation of Claudius looks unconvincing but is not impossible, since Claudius made so much of his campaign in Britain that its loss would have seriously discredited his successor.

The revolt was a set-back to the material development of Britain, which had not gone far by 60. Only Camulodunum possessed the aspect of a Roman town; Londinium and Verulamium were unplanned agglomerations of houses, shops and warehouses. Little had been done to induce the majority of the inhabitants to form new settlements. The tribal nobility certainly suffered in some cases, both from the revolt and from economic changes involving the transformation of their way of life but in general no doubt survived. The change from Celtic warrior-chief to Romanized landowner was just beginning; a few instances have been found, notably in Hertfordshire, of the replacement between 60 and 70 of Belgic huts by new houses, Roman in plan and material, but extremely simple compared with what came later.

2. THE RHINE–DANUBE FRONTIER

Nero's government took over a strategic concept which had governed policy on the Rhine for over forty years. With the recall by Tiberius of Germanicus Caesar from his campaigns beyond the Rhine, and the abandonment of all hope of permanent conquest to the Elbe, the line of the former river changed from being a supply and base line for advance to being an element of a defended frontier. Legionary and auxiliary troops were stationed along it in fortified positions linked by a road. There was no concept of a defence in depth—it was envisaged that engagements with the enemy would take place in the vicinity of defended positions. It must be emphasized that the Rhine itself was not the main defence; it could be crossed fairly easily, especially above Moguntiacum (Mainz), and the forces available were inadequate to dominate every mile of it. It did, however, make an attack in force against the legionary fortresses a difficult proposition. Besides, the river was patrolled by a Roman fleet, the *Classis Germanica*, and was in effect a Roman, not a German, river.

The disposition of the legions was the same as during the later years of Claudius. In Lower Germany, there were four: V Alauda and XV Primigenia at Vetera (Xanten), XVI at Novaesium (Neuss) and I at Bonna (Bonn). In Upper Germany IV Macedonica and XXII Primigenia were stationed at Moguntiacum and XXI at Vindonissa (Windisch). Auxiliary forts were spaced at intervals of seven to fifteen miles. The permanent stations of the legions posed problems of discipline and morale. It may be supposed that traditional military thinking was firmly opposed to anything in the way of amenities for the troops. However, under Claudius we find stone buildings beginning to replace timber and earth constructions at Vetera, Novaesium and perhaps Vindonissa; Vetera was walled in brick under Nero. These developments anticipated the massive stone-built fortresses of the second century. Also Claudio-Neronian was the development of *canabae legionis*. These were quasi-urban settlements outside the forts in which essential services for the legions were provided: smiths, armourers, bakers and so on. In their economic function, buildings and general character, the *canabae* were essentially military and to be distinguished from the true civil settlements which grew up near some forts. The thoroughly military aspect of the Rhineland is further demonstrated by the fact that Upper and Lower Germany were not provinces in the full sense till the time of Domitian, though their commanders ranked below only the *legatus* of Syria.

Apart from training and patrols, troops were frequently used (and not only in Germany) on major construction works, primarily to keep them occupied. Under Claudius, Corbulo employed the army of Lower Germany on a canal twenty-three miles long connecting the Rhine and Maas, while Curtius Rufus employed Upper German troops in silver-mining near Wiesbaden. In 58 Pompeius Paulinus, commander in Lower Germany, completed an embankment on the left bank of the lower Rhine left unfinished by Drusus some seventy years before. A more ambitious scheme was proposed by Antistius Vetus—a canal to connect the Moselle with the Saône, thus making river communication between the Mediterranean and North Sea possible by way of the Rhone and Rhine. The governor of Belgica, through which part of the canal would run, urged that it would disturb the Gauls and the project was dropped.

In places, the Romans kept the Germans away from the right bank. About 56 the Frisii (their name survives in Friesland), who had had their territory limited by Corbulo in 47, began to expand outside into a strip of land opposite Vetera which the legions used no doubt for pasture. Their chieftains Verritus and Malorix were ordered to leave but allowed to go to Rome to ask for new lands elsewhere. They were given Roman citizenship but the tribe had to be driven out by force. Subsequently another tribe, the Ampsivarii, who had been driven out of their own tribal area by their neighbours the Chauci, occupied the vacant land. Their chief

Boiocalus reinforced his plea with the argument that he had served in the Roman army under Tiberius and Germanicus and kept his tribe friendly to Rome. The governor Duvius Avitus turned down his request though he offered land to Boiocalus in person. The latter rejected the offer and turned to the Bructeri, Tencteri and other tribes for help. The governors of both Germanies promptly crossed the river and deterred the tribes from helping Boiocalus. The Ampsivarii were forced to wander from tribe to tribe seeking in vain for new territory until they lost their tribal identity.

The incidents illustrate several factors which made the Roman position on the Rhine a strong one. Inter-tribal wars were frequent, and the defeated found little support. Conversely, a solid anti-Roman alliance was never achieved. The reasons for the perpetual movements of the tribes which so impressed the Romans are obscure. It appears that their social structure in which the warrior was supreme required that difficulties of over-population or declining fertility of the relatively limited cultivated areas were solved by war and migration rather than by the laborious clearing and settlement of the vast areas of forest. The Romans were often able (though not in the instances in Nero's principate) to play one tribe against another or otherwise induce chieftains to be friendly to Rome.

On the other hand the Germans continued to be regarded as a formidable threat to the Empire, no doubt partly because of the defeat of Varus and Germanicus' lack of success. The conventional wisdom of the age constantly referred to their martial prowess, love of independence and inexhaustible manpower. 'Who are more courageous than the Germans? Who are bolder in a charge? Who have more love of the arms to which they are born and bred, and which are their concern to the exclusion of everything else? Who are more hardened to all kinds of endurance since they are for the most part provided with no protection for their bodies and with no shelter against the continual rigour of the climate?' (Seneca, *De Ira* I, 11). A number of

Germans were in the Roman service. Auxiliary units at this time were largely recruited on the spot, and some tribes on the left bank were German. Particularly important were the Batavians, living within the Empire in the Rhine delta but apparently in a special category. They were subject to a levy and in Nero's time provided no less than 10,000 men, who were a formidable threat when they revolted in 69. A substantial part of the *Classis Germanica* was also manned by Germans.

The conquests of Caesar and Augustus, which had brought the boundary of the Empire to the Rhine and Danube, naturally made Italy safer than ever before from attack from the north. It is nevertheless astonishing with what confidence the area from Vindonissa, near Basle, to Carnuntum, near Vindobona (Vienna) on the Danube, was judged not to need a legion. The provinces of Raetia and Noricum, in effect outposts of Italy, were governed by men of equestrian rank, and the auxiliary cohorts which formed the military force at their disposal were not moved to the line of the Danube till the time of Claudius. These limited dispositions were made possible by the lack of any formidable tribe in the Black Forest and the decline of the power of the Marcomanni, previously a strong German people to the north of the upper Danube.

Carnuntum was held by XV Apollinaris till 63 when it was replaced by X Gemina from Spain. In the province of Moesia on the lower Danube there were generally three legions, though their locations are not certain for Nero's principate. The most westerly was probably Viminacium (Kostolac) held by VII Claudia Pia Fidelis from 57 at the latest; next came Oescus (Gigen) where V Macedonica was stationed till it was moved to the East in 61–62, to be replaced in 68 by III Gallica from Syria. Novae (Svistow) was probably the station of VIII Augusta. There was also one legion (XII Gemina) at Poetovio (Pettau) in Pannonia and another (XI Pia Fidelis) at Burnum (Kistanje) in Dalmatia.

These six legions were a smaller total for a much

larger area than that defended by the legions on the Rhine. The relative strength of the forces in the two areas changed later in the first century, and the threatening movements of nomadic tribes which caused the change occurred in Nero's principate. The Sarmatians and their kin the Scythians, both more or less Iranian in language-grouping, had for centuries lived a semi-nomadic pastoral life in the steppes beyond the Sea of Azov, the Caucasus and the Caspian. During the first century, the most powerful of the Sarmatians were the Alani, the centre of whose power lay north of the Caucasus. Other Sarmatian tribes were moving westwards, presumably under pressure from movements in central Asia which cannot now be identified. Following the path to the Danube came the Roxolani (Blond Alani); about 62, in conjunction with the Dacians and the Bastarnae (a Germanic tribe) they formed some sort of threat to the lower Danube. The sepulchral inscription of the then *legatus* of Moesia, Plautius Silvanus, records his achievements:

> He brought more than 100,000 Transdanubian natives across the river with their kings and chieftains, wives and children, to pay tribute; he checked the movement of the Sarmatians, although he had sent a large part of his army to the Armenian campaign; kings unknown before or hostile to Rome he brought to the river bank to pay homage to the Roman standards; he returned to the kings of the Bastarnae, the Roxolani and the Daci their captured sons or brothers and received hostages, consolidating and extending the peace of the province (Smallwood, 228).

It may be supposed that Silvanus campaigned across the Danube, though if there had been major battles they would have been mentioned. The transplanting of a substantial population had its precedent in the time of Augustus; whether in either case the tribes were requesting admission to the Empire because of pressure from enemies (as frequently happened in later centuries) is not known; there appears to be no archaeological evidence of settlement of the Roxolani west of the Dniester in the first century which would prove such pressure, but their raids were widespread and destructive. The settlement in Roman territory was advantageous to the Empire; Moesia was underpopulated, and Silvanus' further claim that he was the first governor of the province to send a substantial contribution to the food supply of the city of Rome is significant. Peace on the Danube was short lived, however; in the winter of 67–68 there was an attack across the river by the Roxolani resulting in the loss of a couple of Roman cohorts, and in 69 a force of 9,000 crossed in a large scale looting expedition, to be followed by the Dacians. The latter tribe again became a formidable threat in the principate of Domitian.

3. THE ARMENIAN PROBLEM

Throughout the Julio-Claudian period, the military establishment of Syria was four legions and a full complement of auxiliaries. They were concerned with the internal security of the province, which was one of the richest in the Empire, but liable to raids from the mountains and desert, and with the numerous client-states to the north and south of Syria, still important in the time of Nero. It is not surprising that the Syrian legate was the highest ranking of imperial commanders. The stations of the legions are not certain, but they were all in or near cities; probably Antioch, Cyrrhus (Khoros), Laodicea (Latakia) and Raphaneae (Rafniyeh) were the stations of III Gallica, X Fretensis, VI Ferrata and XII Fulminata. It became a commonplace, probably justified, to say that the legions of Syria were inferior in discipline and morale to those of the northern armies because of their comfortable billets. One reason for their stations was the lack of a suitable frontier region of defined character where the province bordered the desert. Furthermore, at this date there was no legionary camp at any crossing of the Euphrates, though there were customs posts for the substantial duties exacted

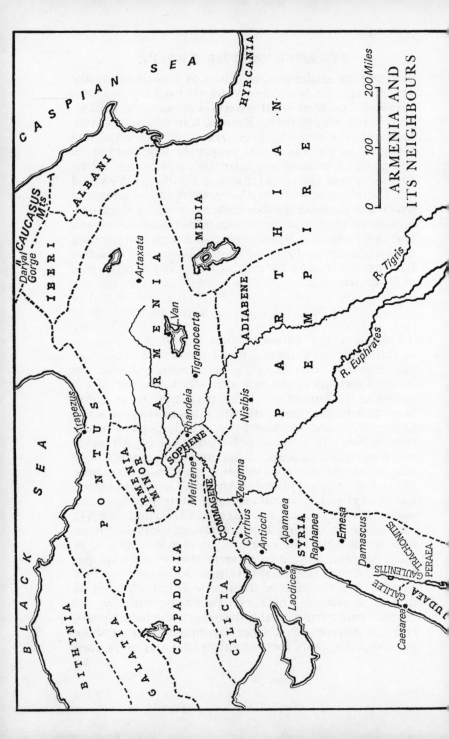

ARMENIA AND
ITS NEIGHBOURS

CASPIAN SEA

BLACK SEA

HYRCANIA

CAUCASUS Mts.
Daryal Gorge

IBERI

ALBANI

MEDIA

ARMENIA

• Artaxata

Van

• Tigranocerta

PARTHIAN EMPIRE

ADIABENE

R. Tigris

R. Euphrates

PONTUS

Trapezus

Rhandeia

Nisibis

SOPHENE

ARMENIA MINOR

Melitene

Zeugma

BITHYNIA

GALATIA

CAPPADOCIA

COMMAGENE

Cyrrhus

• Antioch

Apamaea

SYRIA

Raphanea

• Emesa

Damascus

CILICIA

Laodicea

GALILEE

GAULANITIS

PERAEA

TRACHONITIS

JUDAEA

• Caesarea

0   100   200 Miles

from the eastern trade. The lack of a legionary force on the river gives a clue to the strategic assumptions underlying another notable feature of the eastern situation, which was that the Romans felt able to face the Parthian Empire, the only existing state with which the Roman Empire could be compared, with only four legions. The assumptions were that on the whole the Parthians were not a threat to the Roman Empire, and that there was a good case for not stationing legionary troops in an unnecessarily advanced position on the Parthian frontier. The screen of client-states which the Romans long maintained had the advantage of minimizing direct contact between the powers, besides administrative convenience.

These assumptions were not those with which the Romans first encountered the Parthians, nor were they undisputed. In the principate of Nero, the strategies of both Empires were tested in a military and diplomatic encounter which we know in more detail than most in Roman imperial history, and which had important consequences. It is necessary therefore to outline the earlier relations between the two powers.

In the last decades of the Republic, the spirit of Roman imperialism, conscious of a destiny to create by force of arms a protectorate over the entire known world, was at its most aggressive, and the Parthian Empire appeared no more formidable than other powers conquered by the Romans. The defeat of Crassus' invasion of Parthia in 53 B.C. did not change this view but merely led to repeated demands for revenge. This was never achieved, largely because of the Roman civil wars, though Julius Caesar was planning to lead sixteen legions against Parthia when he was assassinated; in 37–36 B.C. Antony actually undertook an invasion with 100,000 men but had to retreat after suffering heavy losses.

The situation faced by Augustus after he had established his position was that two Roman invasions of Parthia had been disastrous, while the Parthians had had just as little success in an attack on Rome's eastern provinces. It had probably become clear, as knowledge of the East grew, that the Parthian state was formidable in defence of its own territory but was not in a position to threaten the Roman Empire. The Parthian kings were theoretically despots, but they ruled over a fractious hereditary nobility whose obligations to their king are obscure and were certainly often ignored. Revolts and civil wars were frequent as the royal harems produced a continuing supply of potential usurpers, the only fixed principle of succession being, it would seem, that a member of the Arsacid house should rule. The army consisted largely of levies raised by the nobles. Its strength was in its cavalry, especially on its own ground, but it lacked the training and discipline of the Romans, was ineffective in siege warfare, and could not be maintained in the field for any length of time.

Augustus was able to spend the first decade of his rule on important tasks in the West, confident that four or five legions in Syria were an adequate defence in the East. Only in 23 B.C., with popular opinion still strong for retaliation against Parthia, was the demand for the return of captives and lost standards reiterated. The mere threat of an invasion was enough, and in 20 B.C. king Phraates returned them.

Augustus was aware that opinion in Rome had expected more than a diplomatic success and he tried to give the impression that Parthia and Armenia were clients of Rome, but the reality was very different even in Armenia. The position of the latter country—the Poland of the ancient East—was such that its independence was bound to be limited by one or other of its more powerful neighbours. The aristocracy was Iranian in religion, language and custom, and thus more inclined to Parthia, and every decade showed the difficulty experienced by a client-king in the Roman interest; yet the Parthians too had trouble when they were in the ascendency, such was the strength of the feeling for Armenian independence, or rather freedom of action by its aristocracy. As for Parthia, the equality of the two powers was recognized in Augustus' own lifetime; for example, in 1, his grandson Gaius had a personal meeting with the Parthian king on an island in the middle of the Euphrates, thus on neutral ground, and elaborate protocol stressed the equal power of the two Empires; this admission of equality was reflected in the literature of the generation of Augustus.

Furthermore, although Augustus was able on a number of occasions to install nominees on the Armenian throne (and once on the Parthian) Rome gained little real power. He made little or no effort to back them up; once installed they were on their own. On no less than four occasions in his principate the Armenians rejected his nominees. Remarkable though it appears, there seems to have been an accepted convention that such rejections constituted in principle no loss of Roman prestige; whether efforts would be made to restore clients depended on specific factors at the time—and in fact they were rarely made. This was bound up with the want of a large striking force in the East. The fact is that Augustus' decision to fix the total number of legions in the Empire at twenty-eight, followed by long years of effort in Germany, not to mention the Pannonian revolt, made the prospect of a major campaign in the East a daunting one. The vast armies of the last decades of the Republic were strictly phenomena of a political crisis, intolerable for any length of time to the citizen population of Italy and to the provincials, and a political danger to the emperor. The sixteen legions which Caesar planned to lead against Parthia, and the same number actually used by Antony, were simply not available to Augustus.

In the generation after the death of Augustus there was no significant change, as Tiberius strictly followed the policy of his predecessor. In 47 a Parthian embassy came to ask Claudius to send them as king Meherdates, son of Augustus' unsuccessful claimant Vonones. Tacitus (*Annals* XII, 10 and 11) makes the Parthian envoys refer to 'your long established and recognized alliance with us, and your obligation to help allies who equal you in power but admit to second place out of respect'. Claudius in his turn referred to Roman supremacy and Parthian homage. These no doubt traditional gambits were followed by a broad hint from Claudius that Rome found the frequent changes of kings among her eastern neighbours tiresome and wished they would be more stable. This was a logical extension of Augustus' policy. Meherdates was sent out, but Claudius, like Augustus and Tiberius, gave his nominee no help and he soon fell. Subsequently the throne passed to a collateral Arsacid line in the person of Vologaeses. This prudent ruler made one brother king of Media and in 52 attempted to install another, Tiridates, in Armenia. The opportunity was presented when a revolt against the king of Armenia, Mithridates, was led by his nephew Radamistus, son of Pharasmanes, king of Iberia in the Caucasus. The Romans had some cohorts in Armenia, but when Mithridates fled to one of them, the prefect handed him over to Radamistus for a bribe.

The situation was entirely changed by the intervention of the Parthians in 52 or 53. Radamistus and his Iberians fled without giving battle, and Artaxata and Tigranocerta fell to the Parthians. During an exceptionally severe winter the latter had to withdraw, and Radamistus reoccupied his kingdom, only to be driven out almost immediately in an insurrection, presumably in the interest of Tiridates. Before this had happened Roman troops had been recalled from Armenia 'in case a Parthian war should be provoked'. Obscure though much of what followed is, there is no doubt that the Roman commanders were always under the strictest instructions when it came to actions which might involve a full scale war with the Parthians.

The news of the flight of Radamistus and the second occupation of Armenia by Tiridates reached Rome soon after the death of Claudius, and the new government reacted strongly. It may be supposed that under either government Radamistus would ultimately have been recognized if he had been successful; Tiridates was a different matter. It was one thing for Roman nominees to fail to hold their own in Armenia but quite another for the country to fall under direct Parthian control.

There had been a precedent in 34 when Tiberius had prevented the installation in Armenia of a son of the Parthian king. Nero's government, with the high hopes surrounding it at the start, could attempt no less.

The task of recovering Armenia was allotted early in 55 to the consular Cn. Domitius Corbulo, with control over the provinces of Cappadocia and Galatia and the title of *legatus Augusti propraetore*. Corbulo had a high military reputation, though as usual in this period it was based on his strict discipline rather than important victories. The legions were brought up to strength and III Gallica and VI Ferrata transferred from Syria to Cappadocia (where there were no legionary troops). Client-kings were mustered—Antiochus IV of Commagene and Herod Agrippa II, ruler of part of Galilee and areas east of Jordan. Lesser Armenia, an ill-defined area separated from Armenia proper by the upper reaches of the Euphrates, was handed over to Herod's cousin Aristobulus, and the neighbouring territory of Sophene to Sohaemus, a member of the ruling dynasty of Syrian Emesa.

Tiridates remained in Armenia, however, undisturbed by Corbulo for several years. This was attributed by Tacitus to the total demoralization found by Corbulo in his legions, but diplomacy may have been tried unsuccessfully. Corbulo also obtained a third legion, X Fretensis, which was replaced in Syria by IV Scythica from Moesia. In 58 active operations began after a winter in training probably near Erzerum. Antiochus attacked the territory opposite Commagene while Caucasian tribes raided from the north. Tiridates protested that this was a breach of friendship between Parthia and Rome which the latter would regret. Corbulo, who knew that Vologaeses was occupied with a revolt of the Hyrcanians to the south-east of the Caspian, rejected the protest and urged Tiridates to petition Nero for recognition.

This was the solution ultimately adopted, but after a number of changes of fortune. The considerations behind the Roman strategy are not explained by

Tacitus, nor does he make clear who was responsible for the change of policy—Nero himself, Corbulo, or other advisers. He may have been uninterested, but more probably simply did not know. A case can be made out for Corbulo, though the impression given by Tacitus that he had freedom of action is no doubt deceptive. If Claudius' hint about Roman dislike of the instability in the East represented a well-supported opinion in Rome, the idea of accepting a Parthian nominee in Armenia as likely to promote stability could have been advocated again in the years since Nero's accession. Vologaeses, however, refused to allow Tiridates to make the concession of acknowledging Rome's formal supremacy in Armenia. The campaign continued, and after the fall of Artaxata, Tiridates fled. The following year Corbulo made the long march south-westwards past Lake Van to take the second capital, Tigranocerta. In 60 an attempt by Tiridates at a counter-invasion was easily defeated and resistance ended.

The flight of Tiridates and his rejection of the proposal to petition Nero for installation as king of Armenia led Rome to revert to the traditional policy of installing a Romanized or Hellenized prince, on this occasion Tigranes, nephew of one of Augustus' unsuccessful nominees. Antiochus, Aristobulus, Pharasmanes and Polemo of Pontus, through whose capital Trapezus (Trebizond) ran an important supply route to Armenia, were given an interest in the new settlement by being allotted tracts of Armenian territory. Corbulo himself took over the province of Syria, leaving 1,000 legionaries and some auxiliaries in Armenia.

With the defeat of the Parthian attempt to install their nominee, the Romans considered the trouble to be over. But in 61 Tigranes began to attack Adiabene, a dependency of Parthia. It seems most unlikely that the Romans approved the action, and Roman troops certainly took no part. History has a sufficiency of examples of client-states who presume too much on the support of their masters when pursuing their own interests, and it is unnecessary to assume an ingenious Roman plot. For

Vologaeses the matter was vital. Under pressure from the Parthian nobility, he made peace with the Hyrcanians, sent Tiridates with a substantial cavalry escort and levies from Adiabene to counter-attack, and himself threatened the Euphrates crossings into Syria to deter Corbulo from sending help to Armenia.

Corbulo wrote to Nero saying that the defence of Armenia needed a separate command in view of the danger to Syria, but meantime sent IV Scythica and XII Fulminata, instructing their commanders to act with discretion. The rest of his troops and provincial levies were moved up to the Euphrates to face the Parthians. Tacitus says (*Annals* XV, 3) 'he preferred to have a war on his hands than to wage it', but gives no reason for this hostile remark. The need for a separate command was obvious from his own appointment in 54 and it was the fact that Syria was more important than Armenia. Tigranes was besieged in Tigranocerta, but Tiridates failed to take it, while Vologaeses ran short of supplies for his cavalry at Nisibis. Corbulo demanded that the siege of Tigranocerta be raised, threatening a counter-invasion of Mesopotamia. Vologaeses, 'who had a fixed and long-established policy of avoiding war with Rome' (Tacitus, *Annals* XV, 5), gave way. He agreed to withdraw Tiridates, and to send a mission to Rome asking for Armenia and a firm peace, which went some way to accepting the proposals of 58. The Roman troops who had been sent to Armenia were also withdrawn and with them, it seems, Tigranes, who does not appear again. There was criticism in Rome at this withdrawal, said to be due to a secret agreement made by Corbulo with the Parthians, but it is not clear that this was so.

Vologaeses' embassy was a failure, though the reasons are not known, and further conflict was inevitable. In 62 Caesennius Paetus, one of the consuls of 61, arrived in Cappadocia, and V Macedonica was sent from Moesia to join the two legions already there. Tacitus, who is hostile to Paetus, says that he boasted that he would turn Armenia into a province, but according to Dio his mandate was defensive, and it was certainly the Parthians who resumed the war by entering Armenia. Paetus failed to save Tigranocerta and fell back on a base camp at Rhandeia to the north of the river Arsenias.

Corbulo's impressive defence of the Syrian frontier where it was marked by the Euphrates included a bridgehead on the further bank, probably opposite Zeugma. According to Tacitus this deterred Vologaeses from attacking Syria, but there was more to it. Vologaeses seems to have been so confident that Corbulo had instructions to avoid direct conflict and would not use the bridgehead for a thrust into Parthia that he concentrated all his efforts in Armenia and besieged Paetus at Rhandeia. Paetus asked for help from Corbulo, who sent 8,000 men. Tacitus alleges deliberate delay, but Corbulo could hardly be blamed for believing that a Roman legionary camp could not possibly be stormed by the Parthians. In fact, Vologaeses was on the point of giving up when Paetus lost his nerve. He concluded a truce with Vologaeses; the Romans would withdraw from Armenia and Vologaeses would again approach Nero for the recognition of Tiridates.

This was a grievous setback to Rome, but Vologaeses had prudently not inflicted such humiliating losses in battle on the Romans as to make a major war inevitable. Corbulo came to meet Paetus and rejected the suggestion of a joint counter-invasion of Armenia on the grounds that this would go beyond his instructions. Instead he returned to Syria and, on the Euphrates bridge, the middle of which was removed, met a Parthian envoy who demanded the withdrawal of the Roman bridgehead across the Euphrates. Corbulo said this could be done provided that the Parthians left Armenia, and the Parthians agreed.

The state of affairs in the East was not known at Rome till the arrival of Parthian envoys, who said that though they had in fact won Armenia in war, Tiridates would do reverence before the Roman standards and the imperial image; he was only prevented from coming to Rome in person by a religious observance which forbade him to cross the sea. The compromise was rejected, and preparations made for war, but it was made clear that the whole affair would be settled if only Tiridates came in person. Corbulo was given extended command over all the forces of the East, with *imperium* superior to all the other governors. Yet another legion, XV Apollinaris, was sent to the East, making seven in all, four of which were led by Armenia. The massive preparations had their effect before he had gone far. A meeting with Tiridates at Rhandeia was arranged—no doubt the Roman defeat was to be cancelled by the acquiescence of the Parthian. Tiridates laid his royal diadem before an image of Nero and promised not to resume it except from the emperor's own hand. Mutually impressive parades, religious ceremonies and feasts provided a gratifying atmosphere of cordiality. Finally, leaving his daughter as a hostage, he returned to Parthia to prepare for his journey to Rome. This did not take place till 66. Meanwhile at least one legion is known to have remained in Armenia, and Corbulo retained his command. The agreement gave Nero the opportunity to close the temple of Janus, a rarely used symbol of the existence of general peace on land and sea. The ceremony was recorded on the coinage of 66, and perhaps repeated.

The visit of Tiridates was an important event in Nero's principate, and much impressed contemporaries. Nero made it the occasion of the most elaborate displays of pageantry and ostentation. The prince was accompanied by an entourage of Parthian notables and 3,000 cavalry, and also a number of Romans including Corbulo's son-in-law Annius Vinicianus. The cost to the Roman treasury was eight hundred thousand sesterces a day, and Pliny says, no doubt rightly, that it was a heavy burden on the provinces. The journey by land took nine months. Nero received the party at Naples; after lavish games at Puteoli they moved on to Rome. A pompous ceremony was held in the Forum in which Nero, in triumphal robe, was accompanied by Senate and praetorians. Tiridates did obeisance to the emperor and the words of Dio (LXIII, 5) may approximate to the original: 'Lord, I am the descendant of Arsaces, brother of the kings Vologaeses and Pacorus, and your slave. I have come to you, my god, worshipping you as Mithras.' Nero replied, ' You have acted well in coming to me so that in person you may experience my grace. I now grant you what your father did not bequeath to you nor your brothers maintain after giving you; I make you king of Armenia that you and they may know that I have the power both to take away and to bestow kingdoms.' The decorations of gold in the theatre, where celebrations were held, and throughout the city were such that the day was popularly called 'Golden Day'. Tiridates is said to have received gifts worth two hundred million sesterces and many skilled workers to rebuild Artaxata, which was to be renamed Neronia. He hired additional workers as well, but the prudent Corbulo later prevented these from leaving the Empire. Overcoming his religious scruples, Tiridates made the return journey by sea to Dyrrhachium and thence to the cities of Asia.

The bearing of Tiridates was impressive and could be contrasted by the malicious with that of Nero, who insisted on demonstrating his powers as a lyre player and charioteer, to the Parthian's disgust (it was said). 'Master, you have a good slave in Corbulo,' he remarked on one occasion, sensibly enough; this was interpreted to mean that he was surprised at Corbulo's continued loyalty. Another remark was remembered, no doubt as seeming odd to the Romans: 'It is not fair to hit a man when he is down.'

Vologaeses had been concerned lest Tiridates suffer humiliation on his journey to Rome. Tacitus was critical (*Annals* XV, 31): 'Being used to barbarian ostentation, he did not understand that among the Romans real power, not its shadow, is valued.' But in the final result of the long dispute, it was the Parthians who obtained the real power and the Romans who had to put up with the shadow. Nevertheless, no criticism of the solution appears in the sources, although Corbulo is treated as a hero and it would have been easy to imply that he could have won important victories if he had not been held back by a cowardly emperor. The solution was justified by a long period of stability, even though Nero's invitation to Vologaeses to follow Tiridates to Rome was rejected—the king sensibly pointed out that it was much easier for Nero than for him to cross the sea; let Nero come to Asia and a meeting could easily be arranged.

It is easy to forget that in all his years in the East, Corbulo never had to fight a major battle. His strength was in his patience; long periods of training and efficient arrangements for supply were prerequisites of any major operation. He showed an excellent appreciation of the military strength needed for a particular operation—perhaps erring on the side of safety; he was obviously persuasive, but Nero deserves credit for continuing to back him with reinforcements. Still more notable was the position he was allowed to retain for eleven years—the command of more troops and a wider territory than had been allowed to any one not of the imperial family since the days of Augustus. In spite of the uncertainties of the narrative and the fact that in war and diplomacy things never go strictly according to plan, the relatively sophisticated handling of the dispute by both sides is certain. Both Rome and Parthia were determined not to go to war with each other directly, and did not regard limited engagements by their troops in Armenia as equivalent to open conflict. Thus the unfortunate Armenians bore the brunt. A substantial element of bluff entered into it, and in Vologaeses the Romans met their match. The Parthian, appreciating that Roman reluctance matched his own, proved a diplomatic master from an inherently weaker military position.

Although the agreement seemed a satisfactory conclusion, the attention of the Romans continued to be directed towards the East. Only after the death of Corbulo, it seems, was III Gallica sent to Moesia and XV Apollinaris to Egypt. In addition, the importance of the Black Sea had been demonstrated; Corbulo had been heavily dependent for supplies on the sea route from the Hellespont to Trapezus. It appeared essential that the kingdom of Pontus, a narrow strip of territory between

Armenia and the Black Sea, be firmly held by Rome. Accordingly, the kingdom was taken over in 64; the new territory was added to the province of Galatia, which now stretched eastwards beyond Batum to the western end of the Caucasus. The bodyguard of the former king Polemo was given Roman citizenship and formed into an auxiliary cohort, and his fleet was incorporated into the Roman naval force on the Black Sea. This fleet numbered forty ships early in Vespasian's principate, and was useful in his cause in 69.

On the northern shore of the Black Sea, it had long been Roman policy to maintain a client-ruler over the mixed population of the kingdom of Bosporus, in the Crimea. The old Greek colonies there had long since lost their independence, and their populations had mingled with their Sarmatian neighbours. Nevertheless the kingdom remained an outpost of civilization worth protecting from attacks by the Scythians and other enemies. It was of some help to the Romans in checking piracy in the Black Sea and had for centuries been an important source of food for the Greek cities of the Aegean. Under Claudius, one of its rulers, Mithridates, had tried to make himself independent of Rome and had been replaced by his half-brother Cotys, who ruled at least till 62. About this time the movements of the Roxolani and other tribes which affected the Danube area had repercussions in the Crimea; the legate of Moesia who had been successful on the Danube, Plautius Silvanus, intervened in the Crimea to relieve Heraclea Chersonensis (near Sebastopol) which was under pressure from the Scythian king. It is possible that from this date, and at any rate from the time of Vespasian, a legionary detachment was stationed in the kingdom, but it was not provincialized; Cotys' son Rhescuporis is attested as king in 67.

At the end of his principate Nero was planning an expedition to the Daryal Gorge which runs through the central Caucasus. Contemporaries called the pass the 'Caspian Gates', incorrectly believing it was a pass famous in the story of Alexander the Great. Nero raised a new legion from selected Italian recruits at least six feet tall which he called 'Alexander's phalanx'; it seems that like many emperors he succumbed to the magic of the great conqueror's name and wished to tread in his footsteps. A further objective was the tribe of the Albani on the western shore of the Caspian between Armenia and the Caucasus. A serious motive was to bar the major routes across the Caucasus against the Sarmatians of the steppes to the north of the mountains—they had already raided south in 35. The Daryal Gorge was the most famous but not the easiest route and nomad movements were just as likely to move along the western shore of the Caspian where the gap between mountain and sea is never less than six miles.

Whether such an expedition, which was prevented by Nero's death, would have been in line with the better relations now established with Parthia may be doubted, even though it soon transpired that defence against the nomads was a real problem. In 72 the Alani raided Media and Armenia, and Tiridates had a narrow escape from being taken prisoner. Subsequently, Vologaeses suggested co-operation in a defence against such raids but this was rejected by Vespasian. Nevertheless, the Romans built a fort at Harmozica near Tiflis, in Iberian territory, which was apparently regarded as an affront by the Parthians, but there were no hostilities. Josephus, writing about 75, took it for granted that Vologaeses was determined to stay at peace with the Romans.

The two legions in Egypt, III Cyrenaica and XXII Deiotariana, were employed almost exclusively on internal security, since the defence of Egypt against external enemies was of little difficulty. The Nile Valley was protected by desert to the east and west. On the upper Nile, a frontier zone with a number of forts had been established by Augustus between the first and second cataracts as a protection against incursions from the south. From that time they practically ceased, and in any case the kingdom of Ethiopia (Sudan) seems to have become weaker. There are a number of references to a campaign planned by Nero against the Ethiopians, but it never went beyond an exploratory mission. This went out in 61. Seneca, writing about two years later, refers to two centurions sent by Nero to discover the source of the Nile. The motive is extremely probable in view of Nero's own personal enthusiasms—and of Seneca's. A reference to the expedition in the elder Pliny is complementary to Seneca's note: a unit of praetorian soldiers under a tribune travelled with local help beyond Meroe further than any previous Greeks or Romans. They returned with a map and a report that the territory was poor and thinly inhabited, most of the towns, including Meroe itself, being in decay. The country, it was said, was ruled by a queen 'Candace' (known to be a title, not a name) but there were forty-five kings as well. If the expedition, in addition to its geographical aim, had had the task of reporting on the country's potential revenues, the unattractive picture it presented must have deterred Nero from further action. It is true that he planned to visit Egypt in 64, and though this was put off the plan was still in being in 66; the visit was probably intended to follow his tour of Greece but there is no hint that it had anything to do with military affairs.

4. THE JEWISH REVOLT

The revolt in 66 which led to the destruction of Jerusalem in 70 was one of the most important events in the history of the Jewish people. It occupied a more modest place in the history of the Roman Empire: Judaea was one of its smallest provinces. However, it had its significance for contemporaries because of the importance of the Jewish element in so many cities, the reputation of Jerusalem as a great religious city of the East and the part taken by Vespasian and Titus, future emperors, in the suppression of the revolt. When the Romans annexed Syria in 63 B.C. much of the neighbouring region had been left under client-rulers, and this included Judaea. The special character of the Jewish religion was recognized, though it was not liked, by the Romans; the

Jews were exempt from military levy, and Jews in the Empire were allowed to send their contributions as before to the temple in Jerusalem. The most successful client-king was Herod, who ruled from 37–4 B.C. He was disliked by the orthodox as being an Idumaean by origin (not a true Jew) and because of Greek influence on his court, but at least the country did not pay tribute or have a Roman garrison. On his death his large kingdom was divided; Archelaus, to whom Augustus allotted Judaea, where the majority of Jews lived, ruled so badly that in 6 the Jews and their enemies the Samaritans united in requesting his removal. Augustus made Judaea a province under an equestrian governor. The location of the governor's residence at Caesarea was no doubt a concession to Jewish feelings about Jerusalem. On the other hand the equestrian status of the province and its garrison of only a few auxiliary cohorts (though the legions of Syria were close by), indicates the unimportance attributed to Judaea in the imperial scheme as a whole.

The economic and social divisions in the province were sharp. There seems no doubt that by ancient standards Judaea was over-populated in spite of the fact that migrants frequently left to swell the Jewish communities which existed in every large city in the East. There was a famine after 44, and public works in Jerusalem sometimes had the function of economic relief; about 64, after the completion of work on the temple, the workers had to be found fresh employment in repairing the streets of the city. One of the first actions of the victorious rebels in 66 was the destruction of money-lenders' bonds in the city archives. There was also the phenomenon of the *sicarii*—'Men of the Dagger'—who assassinated and plundered the wealthy and pro-Roman elements. Such divisions, however, existed elsewhere from time to time in the Empire, without giving rise to anything as serious as the Jewish revolt; what made the situation in Judaea unique was the religious fervour which animated most of the people.

The idea that the people of Israel must be a theocracy, acknowledging no lord but Yahweh antedated the

Roman conquest, and in the period of Seleucid weakness from the middle of the second century B.C. a Jewish state had been able to maintain itself in precarious independence under its own kings. Roman rule extinguished even the shadow of independence previously enjoyed. Examples of religious fervour, primarily among the poor, especially in the country, occurred throughout the first century as one prophet or another attempted to lead his followers into the desert, or preached the divine deliverance of Israel. It should be stressed that the 'Messianic hope' (which was known to the Romans) was not simply an expression of anti-Roman feeling and a desire for Jewish independence; it foretold a complete reversal of affairs, with Israel and its rulers exercising world domination. Belief in the divinely ordained position of the Jews was held by nearly all, though with differences of intensity. The major priesthoods were monopolized by a small group of wealthy families who tended to acquiesce in the Roman domination; these were the Sadducees. They were, however, divided among themselves by feuds in the competition for power, and ineffective as a support for Roman rule. The lesser priests and many of the people belonged to the sect of the Pharisees which stood for a strict observance of the law of Moses. In addition there were specialized communities like the Essenes who lived a communal life in the desert, and the Qumran community (if indeed it was not Essene). Throughout the first century the most explicit champions of an independent Jewish state were the Zealots, carrying Pharisaic doctrine to its logical conclusion.

In such circumstances, even the best of administrations would have been resented, and the Roman was very far from that. Yet it was not so much the defects of the individual procurators which mattered as the failure of the Romans to appreciate fully that they were faced with an unique problem in the case of the Jews. The Romans understood the patriotism which resisted conquest by an imperial power, and appreciated the hatred felt for unjust government, even the arguments against imperialism as such; but no other people in their Empire had the same religious impulse animating a permanent desire for independence. Tacitus, for example, who knew the importance of their religion to the Jews, did not understand its political implications, and treated the revolt in the same way as he did that of Boudicca in Britain, namely as a revolt caused by the misdeeds of the procurators. In fact, the disputes between the procurators and the Jews as recorded in the full account of Josephus are nearly all trivial, but that these trivialities caused violent riots and bloodshed even before the great revolt emphasizes the incompatibility of the Roman Empire with Jewish theocratic ideas.

The most serious incident, and one which above all else made harmony impossible, was the proposal of Gaius to have his statue placed in the temple at Jerusalem. It was known that this would certainly lead to total resistance. When Gaius died before the project was accomplished, it was regarded as an act of divine deliverance, but the feelings against Rome hardened. Claudius tried to remedy the position by reconstituting Herod's kingdom and giving it to his friend Agrippa, who ruled it with some success from 41–44. But when in 44 he organized a meeting of five client-kings, which was dissolved by the governor of Syria, Roman suspicions were aroused. On his death later the same year, Judaea was again made a province. His son Agrippa II continued to be favoured by Claudius and Nero, however. He was given a client-kingdom including Gaulanitis and Trachonitis (east of the upper Jordan) in 53 and about 60 Nero added part of Galilee and Peraea, a further territory east of the Jordan. His subjects included many Jews, and he was able to mediate on the Jews' behalf on a number of occasions before he finally failed to prevent the revolt. He had the right to appoint and dismiss the High Priest, which Claudius had given to his father, but this seems to have made little difference.

The procurator in office at Nero's accession was Antonius Felix, brother of Claudius' influential freedman Pallas; he governed from 52–60, an exceptionally long term of office. Tacitus alleges cruelty but is unspecific; he may have been prejudiced by the social origin of Felix. On the whole, Josephus' complaints are of a minor sort. The next two procurators were relatively unimportant; at any rate there were no serious incidents. The final breach came under Gessius Florus; in May of 66 he took seventeen talents from the temple treasury 'for Caesar's needs', as Josephus put it. It was said that the tribute was forty talents in arrears, but the incident was no doubt an example of the financial difficulties of Nero's last years. Seizure of the temple treasure by the Romans was an infringement of the sanctuary which infuriated the orthodox, and riots broke out; Florus retaliated by allowing a cohort to plunder some part of the city. Two further cohorts were brought up and more riots ensued. Florus apparently found his position untenable and withdrew, leaving one cohort at the disposal of the chief priests who promised to try to restore order. Agrippa, who had been in Egypt, hurried back to try to dissuade the mass of the inhabitants from open revolt. His success was only temporary and he was soon driven out of the city. In August, if not before, war was made inevitable when sacrifice for Rome and the emperor in the temple was abolished, and the fortress of Masada, by the Dead Sea, was seized and its Roman garrison wiped out. In Jerusalem itself there was fighting between the peace-party composed of the chief priests and the wealthy elements and those, by now the majority, who were for open war. The latter gained the upper hand when they forced the garrison (reinforced by Agrippa) out of the fortress in the city and obliged it to surrender —the Romans among them were killed. About the same time 20,000 Jews in Caesarea, where there had long been tension between Jews and Greeks, were massacred. This sparked off retaliation not only in Judaea but also in Agrippa's kingdom and even in Syrian communities where Jews were in the majority; these massacres in turn were matched by others in which Jewish minorities in Greek and Syrian communities were attacked. In Alexandria in Egypt the prefect Tiberius Alexander had to use legionary troops to repress the Jews, who were regarded as the instigators of a serious riot.

In the autumn Cestius Gallus, governor of Syria, entered Galilee and Judaea, now largely in revolt, with one legion and many auxiliaries. Having no regular forces with which to oppose him, the Jews could not prevent him reaching the walls of Jerusalem. After trying the defences for a few days, Gallus withdrew (November 66). Josephus considered this inexplicable; even if he has underestimated the danger to Gallus of irregular bands of Jews operating outside the city, the general seems to have shown excessive caution. His withdrawal became a rout as he was harried in the open country, and the Jews captured many weapons of use to them later. This success strengthened the hands of those who were for war, and the chief priests, who had been for peace, now joined the rebels.

It was fortunate for the Romans that good relations with Parthia had been cemented earlier in the year. When Gallus died during the winter, Nero, confident that Parthia would not take advantage of the situation, was able to create a separate command for the Jewish war and allot it most of the Syrian army. Titus Flavius Vespasianus was appointed in February 67, chosen, like Mucianus, the new *legatus* of Syria, because of his humble origin. He took two legions from Antioch (V Macedonica and X Fretensis) and his son Titus collected XV Apollinaris from Egypt; all told, his army must have numbered at least 50,000 men. His plan was to keep his army together as far as possible, while isolating and attacking each Jewish controlled city. There were hardly any engagements in the open, since no Jewish force could hope to oppose such legionary strength. The process of reducing the cities was a slow one, as Vespasian methodically worked his way southward through Galilee. After wintering in Caesarea he found it easy to overrun Samaria, Idumaea (to the south of Judaea) and Peraea, and was already in position around Jerusalem when he received news of the death of Nero.

In Jerusalem itself the fortifications, which were some of the most massive in the east, had been strengthened.

During 67 the manpower available had been increased as the more determined Zealots fled to the capital before the slow advance of Vespasian. The wealthy element, and those who were suspected of wanting to sue for peace, were killed, imprisoned or driven out. Nevertheless there remained dissension in the city because of rivalry amongst the rebel leaders and their ruthless behaviour; the two most important were John of Giscala and Simon bar Giora. The death of Nero in June 68 provided the Jews with a respite of nearly two years, since Vespasian stopped operations as soon as it was known. It is not impossible that from this date he considered the chances of an attempt on the imperial position if circumstances in the West became favourable; he composed long-standing differences with Mucianus, who was to be his closest adviser.

Minor campaigns round Jerusalem where Simon had been operating took place in the summer of 69, but these must have been to clear the decks for Vespasian's proclamation on 1 July which had been carefully planned over a period of several months. The command was handed over to his son Titus who, with his forces depleted by the despatch of detachments to support the cause of Vespasian, began the siege in the spring of 70. After a determined resistance of some four months the city fell and was completely sacked. The temple itself was destroyed. Resistance continued in a few isolated strongholds till the fall of Masada in 73.

The slaughter and devastation in Judaea had been immense. The temple was deliberately destroyed and the High Priesthood and Sanhedrin (council of chief priests) were abolished in order to deprive the Jews of a national centre even under Roman rule. Nevertheless the separate existence of the Jewish people and religion continued to be recognized, even in the humiliating rule that the contribution which Jews everywhere had previously sent to the temple in Jerusalem must go to the temple of Jupiter Capitolinus (in effect the Roman treasury). The traditional exemptions from military service and the imperial cult continued, together with freedom of worship for local synagogues. The importance of the Jews of the Diaspora increased still further as a result of later revolts in the second century, but they did not forget Jerusalem and its temple.

9
Nero, the Philhellene Emperor

THE crimes of Nero within his own family had provoked no reaction till the outbreak at the divorce of
Octavia, which was easily quelled; in the long run they
probably played only a modest part in alienating
opinion from him. More important in bringing about
this alienation was Nero's rejection of the accepted standard of respectable and dignified behaviour not merely
for an emperor and senator but for the great majority of
Roman citizens (that is to say, Italians); only some
elements of the Roman population remained enthusiastic. The stages of this rejection, which can be traced,
culminated in a phase of philhellenism so extreme that
it included not merely a total acceptance of all Greek
culture and an attempt to impose Greek patterns on
the traditional brutal Roman amusements—a not un-
commendable objective—but a desire to live the life
and enjoy the esteem of a popular performer on the
stage in a Greek environment. This sort of behaviour
aroused the strongest feelings of repulsion among substantial elements in the Senate, equestrian order and
Italy generally who, whatever their faults, regarded
the government of the Roman Empire as a serious
matter.

The attitude of the Romans to the Greeks and Greek
civilization was notoriously ambivalent. From the early
second century B.C. they had been exposed to it in so
many ways that no one could imagine Rome untouched
by the influence of things Greek. Every educated Roman
admitted the primacy of Greece in almost all branches
of literature and the arts. Yet at the same time Greek
influence was frequently regarded as demoralizing or
subversive or both. The same conventional attitudes
were expressed by reasonably enlightened men such as
the younger Pliny at the beginning of the second century

A.D. as three centuries before by the elder Cato. In imperial Rome, it was admittedly no longer possible to regard Greek influence, with the exception of Stoic philosophy (see below, p. 143), as subversive, but we observe a continuing resistance. If in the course of time one object of criticism became accepted, another was soon found. The opposition was reinforced by the political subjection of the Greeks, which seemed to demonstrate that primacy in the arts was not enough, and by their habit of harping on ancient glories, which inevitably made their political decline more obvious. To condemn something new as Greek was for long the last resource of Roman contempt.

Augustus, though bound to a degree by his early propaganda which represented his war against Antony and Cleopatra as the cause of Roman tradition against the corruption of the Hellenistic East, was after all an educated Roman. He was extremely fond of Greek literature and a friend of a number of Greek scholars, though he never ventured, unlike many educated Romans, to write in the language. The political supremacy of Rome and Italy which dominated his conception of the Roman Empire implied no positive hostility to the Greek world. In fact the Greeks of Asia benefited more than most from the establishment of peace and order. Furthermore, his particular interest in the cult of Apollo, admittedly in Latin form, implied a positive attitude to the deity who above all others symbolized the essence of Greek civilization. It was thus possible for Nero to associate the memory of Augustus with some at least of his pursuits. He laid before the statue of Augustus the crowns which he was awarded at the festival at the dedication of his gymnasium in 62, and took part in the Actian games at Nicopolis which had been established by Augustus to celebrate his victory at Actium. On the birth of his daughter Claudia the Senate decreed games on the model of another Actian festival established by Augustus in Rome. This Roman festival was on a Greek, not Roman, pattern, but it had apparently ended with Augustus' death.

In the imperial house itself, there had been certain individuals with an interest in Greek above the average. The most important was no less than Nero's grandfather Germanicus. In addition to his military and political activities under Augustus, Germanicus was the writer of comedies and epigrams in Greek and the translator of the Greek poet Aratus' *Phaenomena* into Latin. He toured Greece, visited many of the islands and cities of Asia and finally went to Egypt to look at its antiquities, walking about unguarded and in Greek dress. He also allowed a chariot to be raced in his name at Olympia. Germanicus' mother, the younger Antonia, who long survived her son, was also notable. She remained on good terms with the Julian family in spite of being the daughter of Mark Antony, and retained many of her father's eastern connexions. She had estates in Egypt (Alexander Lysimachus, brother of the Jewish scholar Philo and father of Nero's prefect of Egypt, Ti. Julius Alexander, was her agent) and was a friend of the Herods of Judaea and other client-princes. When Gaius, who had spent three years in her household, became emperor, he gave kingdoms to three of his youthful companions whom he had got to know at this period. Gaius had several traits which were paralleled in Nero—admiration for Greek culture, a love of the marvellous and enthusiasm for large building projects. Intellectually he was more acute than Nero, and though, like the latter, not really interested in the work of government, at least saw clearly through the façade of the principate, and when he was assassinated was proceeding rapidly on a course which would have ended with a system much closer to Hellenistic monarchy. It was even alleged that he proposed to take up permanent residence in Alexandria—the thought that the centre of government might be transferred to the East was a recurring fantasy of the Romans. Finally Claudius, who had lived the life of a scholar for many years before becoming emperor, was naturally more serious in his approach. Fluent in Greek, using it frequently even in the Senate when receiving embassies from the Greek world, two of his historical works were written in the language—twenty books on Etruscan history and eight on Carthaginian.

In Nero's case, the traditional education by Greek pedagogues provided him with a basic equipment in Greek, but the fact that he became emperor at seventeen meant that he did not finish his education, as was usual, with a visit to the Greek world and a stay at some school of rhetoric at Athens or Rhodes. Nero's enthusiasm for things Greek was not so much the result of his education, or the influence of a particular teacher, as part of his artistic and intellectual interest in general. Tacitus was not uncomplimentary (*Annals* XII, 3): 'From early boyhood, Nero's lively mind was directed to other pursuits [i.e. other than rhetoric]—carving, painting, singing and riding; at times in his verses he showed that he possessed the rudiments of learning.' Nothing is known of his performance in the visual arts, but he was an enthusiastic collector to an extent that may have diminished his popularity in the Greek world. The provinces of Asia and Achaea were visited by agents of Nero seeking for works of art to bring back to Rome. Such looting expeditions by Roman generals in the days of conquest had been traditional, but the references to Nero's exactions show that the practice had become rare. The finest statues were certainly used in the imperial residences (and were subsequently placed in Roman temples by Vespasian). According to Pausanias, 500 were taken from Delphi alone, certainly a tendentious figure put out by the temple authorities. Elsewhere we hear of famous individual pieces from Olympia and Thespiae. Pergamum also suffered, but Rhodes was spared because of Nero's early association with the political fortunes of the island.

According to Suetonius (*Nero*, 52), 'he composed verses with pleasure and without effort, and did not, as some say, publish those of other writers as his own. Some note-books and loose sheets have come into my hands which contain some of his most famous lines written in his own hand in a way which indicates that they had not been transcribed from a copy or taken down from dictation but were written by the emperor himself for they contain many deletions, alterations and amendments.' Tacitus argued differently (*Annals* XIV, 16): 'Nero gathered around him some who possessed poetical ability but were not well known. They dined together and then collated verses which they had brought with them or composed on the spot, adding them to Nero's own suggestions. This is clear from Nero's poems which lack vigour, inspiration and uniformity of style.' But Nero is not accused elsewhere of plagiarism, and it may be supposed that he was serious about his poetry as he was about his singing.

His literary friends did exist, however. Foremost among them was Seneca's nephew Lucan, only two years Nero's junior. He was honoured with the quaestorship before the minimum age and was still in favour in 60 when he won the first prize at the Neronia (see below, p. 115) with a poem in praise of Nero. Details of their subsequent quarrel are variously recorded, but the superior talents of Lucan and his high regard for his own worth probably made a break with the emperor inevitable. Cocceius Nerva, the future emperor, was called the Tibullus of his age by Nero, and was certainly influential at the time of the Pisonian conspiracy. Fabricius Veiento, exiled for libellous satires in 62, was also accused of abusing his influence with Nero, and was one of Nero's literary friends. Nero may also have patronized Seneca's friend Lucilius.

Only a few lines of his poems have survived, just about sufficient to confirm, what could be guessed, that his taste was entirely that of his age; they could easily be from Lucan or Silius Italicus. His best known work was the *Troica*, an epic on Troy in which Paris was the hero, even defeating Hector in the games. It has been plausibly suggested that Nero was attracted to this version of the legend precisely because of the less conventionally virtuous character of the hero. Nero also projected a vast epic on Rome, which, however, provided no more than an edifying tale about the Stoic philosopher Annaeus Cornutus. 'Even before composing a line of it he began to consider the proper number of books, consulting among others Annaeus Cornutus. . . . While some were urging him to write 400 books, Cornutus said that this was too many and nobody would read them. When someone objected that Chrysippus (the Stoic), whom Cornutus praised and imitated, composed many more, he replied, "Yes, but they were a help to men's lives." For this Cornutus incurred banishment' (Dio, LXII, 29). Nero's favourite parts for his stage performances were Orestes the Matricide, Oedipus Blinded, Hercules in Madness and Canace in Labour. The subjects are akin to or the same as those treated by Seneca in his tragedies, and no doubt Nero's compositions were equally rhetorical. He also wrote minor poems, some of the kind fashionable at the time and exemplified by Martial.

However, Nero's chief loves were and remained singing to his own accompaniment on the lyre and, to an almost equal degree, chariot racing. At the beginning of his principate he took lessons from the leading virtuoso on the lyre, Terpnus by name. His voice was low pitched and rather weak, but throughout his life he devoted much attention to improving it by breathing exercises and herbal medicines, and always avoided any strain on his voice. His addiction to these pursuits seems to have been due in part to his craving for applause, and increasingly to an admiration amounting to envy of the life led by professional performers, free from traditional restraints and conventions. The adulation of the court circle was clearly insufficient for him. He needed the popularity and applause which were accorded to the favourites of the theatre and the circus, and thus came to reject as mere convention the traditions of dignified behaviour as understood by the ruling class in Rome. Yet he was well aware of the dangers involved; opinion in Rome and Italy would tolerate an emperor who was a literary dilettante, but public appearances as a performer in the theatre were shocking except to the Roman proletariat. In the early years there were no public appearances such as those which were later found so offensive.

Tacitus associated Nero's first performances before spectators with the death of Agrippina, probably a correct estimate of the restraining influence of her personality even when she was excluded from power. He attributed the following arguments to the emperor (*Annals* XIV, 14): 'He had long had a desire to participate in four-horse chariot races and a no less disgraceful ambition to sing to the lyre in a professional manner. He argued that chariot racing was an accomplishment of ancient kings and leaders honoured by poets and associated with the worship of the gods. As for singing, it was sacred to Apollo and that glorious and provident deity was represented in a musician's dress in Greek cities and Roman temples.' This was all drawn from Greece; Nero was thinking of the heroes of epic and the many historical examples of the classical Greek period, and the poetry of Pindar and others. His approach was to introduce into Roman society games on the Greek pattern. For a long time, however, in spite of Tacitus' implications, his performances remained semi-private. The private race-course of Gaius in the Vatican valley was enlarged, now being called the *Circus Gai et Neronis*; there he could stage his chariot races before invited spectators. The same year he instituted new games entitled *Juvenalia* (Youth Games), on the occasion of his first shaving his beard, a traditional family festival. The Juvenalia consisted of theatrical and musical performances in both Greek and Latin and were celebrated in his private gardens. It was on this occasion that men of senatorial and equestrian rank first took part.

The strength of upper-class opinion against this was enormous. All the sources denounce the practice; undoubtedly substantial rewards were offered by Nero to those who 'volunteered', but Tacitus regarded appearances as due to social compulsion, since Nero himself played and sang. It appears that persons of high standing also appeared in the amphitheatre at about this time. There were indeed a few precedents of impoverished or publicity-seeking nobles appearing in public under earlier emperors, but there was a senatorial decree of

Augustan date against it. It may be that many of the participants under Nero were of the younger element, but Nero appears to have gone so far as to hope to Hellenize the Roman games entirely. The Juvenalia, which by definition could properly be held only once, were repeated annually at least till 64, as a suitable occasion for Nero's own appearances. A further innovation of Hellenistic type was the formation of a corps of young, wealthy Romans called *Augustiani*. This body was to be part bodyguard, part club of enthusiasts for the new games and part claque for Nero. It had the advantage of involving the young who might be more sympathetic to Nero's ideas. They were trained by cheer leaders in the various techniques of organized rhythmic applause.

In 60 Nero went further. He instituted at Rome a *certamen quinquennale* (Five Yearly Contest), with competitions in 'music' (this included poetry and rhetoric as well as music in our sense), athletics and racing. The institution came to be known as the Neronia because of its special association with the emperor, and was important enough to be celebrated on the coinage. The five-year interval, instead of the four years standard in the games of ancient Greece, was a concession to the Roman tradition of the *lustrum*, a five-year cycle. The games lasted several days and were presided over by men of consular rank drawn by lot. Nero encouraged the educated classes at Rome to take part in the 'music' competitions. Tacitus' indignation is tempered by irony at the excesses of conservative opposition and an admission that the cheerfully prophesied riot of immorality never occurred. It may further be noted that on this genuinely public occasion, Nero did not take part in person, though he did when the *certamen* was repeated in 65. The athletic competitions were still the object of suspicion. Such performances, by Greek professionals, had rarely been seen in Rome, though they had been included in Augustus' Actian games. In 61 Nero built his magnificent gymnasium which was to encourage the upper classes, but the Roman prejudice that only military or para-military exercises were legitimate, and that Greek athletics led to effeminacy and homosexuality, was firmly entrenched.

In the end, performances in his private theatre and grounds were not sufficient. His first truly public appearance occurred in 64, and was associated with plans to appear in a Greek environment. It is probable that he now realized that the strength of feeling in Rome was too strong to be overcome and that the public applause for which he craved must be sought elsewhere. He went to Naples, perhaps because of its Greek origin and performed there in the theatre as a singer to his own accompaniment on the lyre. He then set out for Greece to take part in the ancient festivals, but after going as far as Beneventum returned for some unknown reason to the capital. He next planned a visit to the eastern provinces and in particular Egypt (the Alexandrians were notorious for their devotion to music) but gave this up also. However, in 65 the Neronia were repeated. The Senate, possibly in an attempt to prevent his participating, offered him the prize for poetry and rhetoric in advance. Nero had at first intended to perform only in his garden but 'in accordance with popular request', it was said (Suetonius, *Nero*, 21), he took part with the other competitors in the theatre of Pompey.

The plan to visit Greece was resumed the following year: 'Only the Greeks have an ear for music and are good enough to judge my performance', he is supposed to have remarked (Suetonius, *Nero*, 22). He left Rome at the end of September with an entourage of a number of senators, praetorian soldiers under Tigellinus, and the *Augustiani*. He took part in the Actian games and probably wintered in Corinth. In 67, on his demand, the four great national festivals of Greece were held in the same year so that he could have the opportunity of being *periodonikes*—winner in all the contests. The sequence was probably Olympia, Delphi, Isthmus and Nemea. It need hardly be said that he was awarded the prize not only in the contests in which he took part but in all the others as well. The words of the proclamation on each occasion ran, 'Nero Caesar wins this contest and awards the crown to the Roman people and his own inhabited world.' It is well attested that he took his role as contestant with complete seriousness even though he must have realized his victories were inevitable. Between the contests he toured the country though we have few details of activities outside the religious centres. He attempted to find out the depth of the traditionally bottomless Lake Alcyon, and inaugurated another of his great building projects, a canal through the isthmus of Corinth (see p. 133). He refrained from visiting the two most famous ancient cities of Greece, Athens and Sparta, an omission for which only a fanciful reason could be alleged even in antiquity.

The climax of the visit came in November 67. The Isthmian games (which had probably been celebrated the year before) were repeated where, in 196 B.C., Quinctius Flamininus had proclaimed the freedom of Greece after Rome's defeat of Philip V of Macedon. On the present occasion, Nero announced the restoration of freedom to Achaea in a speech which has survived on an inscription from Acraephia (Karditza) in Boeotia (Smallwood, 64):

> The emperor Caesar says: 'Wishing to thank most noble Hellas for its good will and reverence towards me, I order as many inhabitants of the province as possible to come to Corinth on 28 November.'
>
> When the crowds had gathered in the place of assembly he spoke the following words:
>
> 'Men of Hellas, I give you an unlooked for gift—if indeed anything may not be hoped for from one of my greatness of mind—a gift so great, you were incapable of asking for it. All Greeks inhabiting Achaea and the land called till now the Peloponnese receive freedom and immunity from taxes, something which not all of you enjoyed even in your happiest days; for you were subject to strangers or to each other. I wish I were giving this gift when Hellas was still flourishing so that more people might enjoy the benefit, and I blame time itself

for spending in advance the greatness of my gift. But I am bestowing this benefaction on you not out of pity but out of good will, in recompense to your gods whose care for me both on land and on sea I have never found wanting, and who are affording me an opportunity to bestow so great a benefaction; for other rulers have granted freedom to cities, but Nero alone to an entire province.'

The 'freedom of Greece' was a most evocative phrase in the Greek world which, as the Romans used to complain, was always dreaming of its past glories. The gesture cost Rome little, since the country was poor and could have provided little revenue; conversely, immunity from tribute was a substantial benefit. Politically, 'freedom' was a formality; Athens and Sparta and a number of other Greek communities still enjoyed it. The chief benefit was to be outside a Roman governor's jurisdiction. Achaea had been a senatorial province, and the Senate was compensated by being allotted Sardinia— the arrangement had already been made by the middle of 67. Nevertheless, in spite of its limited effect, Nero's liberation of Greece was long remembered, particularly as it lasted only a few years, being cancelled by Vespasian. It flattered the Greeks that a Roman emperor could be described as philhellene in more than empty formality. For such diverse writers as Pausanias, Plutarch and Philostratus, the gift of freedom to Greece was something substantial to be put in the balance against Nero's crimes and follies. It is certainly true that Pausanias and others remembered and resented the pillage of Greek statues, and no doubt the presence in Greece of so large an entourage was a heavy burden at the time, but evidence that Nero was favourably regarded in the Greek world as a result of the liberation is substantial.

There is an authentic note of megalomania in Nero's pronouncement at the Isthmus, and this can be associated with the tendency in the Greek world to exalt the person of the emperor as a quasi-divine being. It is by no means easy to grasp the nuances and estimate the real significance of the imperial cult. Put briefly, the cult was an expression of loyalty and an acknowledgement of the ruler's overwhelming power. It was clearly more than 'homage' but rather less than 'worship'. Hellenistic kings in Egypt, Syria and Asia had received divine honours from their subjects as had their oriental predecessors, and in almost all cases the impulse came from below and was not imposed from above. When Rome conquered the Greek-speaking part of the Mediterranean, some of her generals were honoured there, but ruler-cult had no place in Rome till Julius Caesar received quasi-divine honours and was declared a god by the Senate after his death. Subsequently, the imperial cult had three main aspects: the official honours paid to a former emperor who had been officially deified, the official honouring of an emperor in his lifetime, and the unofficial honouring of an emperor in his lifetime. The first does not concern us here. In the case of the second, the limits were drawn by Augustus. In view of the strength of Roman opinion against ruler-worship, and all his concessions to Republican forms, it was impossible for him to accept divine honours indiscriminately. Many honours appropriate more to gods than men were voted to him by the Senate, but it was quite clear that in Rome and Italy the emperor was not the object of a cult. In the provinces, especially those in the East, he carefully regulated the honours he received from peoples accustomed to deify their rulers. Temples could be set up by provincial councils, representative of the cities of a province, dedicated in most cases to 'Rome and Augustus', though sometimes to Augustus alone. The same process occurred in western provinces, but much more slowly; Africa had no imperial cult till Flavian times. Any extravagance in the forms of the official cult was rejected. This policy was adhered to by Tiberius and Claudius, though Gaius had begun to insist on being hailed as a god.

Individual cities and private persons could go further. In the West this rarely went beyond the poetical usage which could regularly refer to living emperors as gods.

In the East, however, we have more extravagant expressions and the identification of the ruler with specific deities. At the beginning of his principate, Nero had been hailed by the poets in terms reminiscent of those used of Augustus, and the theme of his association with Apollo was already to be heard. In Alexandria, a reorganization of the units into which the Greek population was divided gave an opportunity for the new units to receive grandiose names, some dynastic and some of quasi-religious significance. Alexandrian local coinage was more direct; Nero is equated with the city's protecting deity as 'the New Good Spirit' and appears on both papyri and inscriptions as 'the New Good Spirit of the Universe'. Again in Egypt he is referred to as 'Saviour and Benefactor of the World'. In a number of local coins in the East, he is called quite simply *theos* (god). Identifications with specific deities become frequent late in his principate; at Athens (a 'free' city) he is 'New Apollo'; coins of Patrae call him 'Hercules Augustus'; he is more than once called the 'New Sun' and on the inscription of Acraephia he is called the 'New Sun who has shone upon Hellas'; the same inscription refers to the setting up of an altar to *Nero Zeus Eleutherios* (Zeus the Liberator). Elsewhere he is also 'New Zeus' and in Cos 'New Asclepius' (the local patron deity).

All these are in the Greek world and most can be associated with his later years, if not his visit to Greece. Although there were precedents—Claudius had been called 'Saviour and Benefactor', a centuries-old designation in the Hellenistic world, and he and Tiberius are both called *theos* on coins—there can be little doubt that the outburst under Nero was a spontaneous reaction to his philhellenism, and also acceptable to the emperor. Dio gives the acclamations, no doubt organized, which greeted Nero on his return to Rome from his Greek visit (LXII, 20): 'Hail Olympian Victor! Hail Pythian Victor, Augustus, Augustus! Hail Nero Hercules, Hail Nero Apollo! The only Victor in all Contests from the beginning of time! Augustus, Augustus! Divine Voice, blessed are they that hear you!'

In the West, signs of a change again came at the end of his principate. Earlier, in 55, his image had been placed in the temple of Mars Ultor; apparently this was the first time since Caesar that an emperor had been so directly associated with a god in Rome. A notable private monument at Moguntiacum, the so-called Jupiter column, is difficult to interpret, and while it certainly glorified Nero, its complex religious message may be associated with the spread of Roman religion in the Rhineland rather than the imperial cult itself. The imperial coinage remained conservative in type till 65; coins celebrating the Armenian victories with the legend *Pace P.R. terra marique parta Ianum clusit* (He closed the temple of Janus after establishing Roman peace on land and sea), and his subsequent escape from the Pisonian conspiracy with *Iuppiter Custos* (Jupiter the Protector) and *Salus* (Safety), were traditional and inoffensive. From 65, however, we have a few coins, all in copper, which go further, depicting Nero wearing the so-called radiate crown, reserved for deified emperors; on the reverse of one issue of these, Nero is identified with Apollo Citharoedus (Apollo the Lyre Player). This was so exceptional that it was noted by Suetonius in one of the very few references to coin-types in ancient literature. It therefore appears that as a result of his breach with the Senate after the conspiracy of Piso, and his experience of the way the Greek world expressed itself, Nero was moving in the same direction as Gaius had done, and was going to base his rule on an undisguised personal power with religious sanction. The colossal statue of himself by the Greek artist Zenodorus, which he had placed in the vestibule of the Golden House, is a further indication; after his death it needed little alteration to be turned into an image of the Sun god.

This is not to say that Nero succumbed to illusions of his own divinity; in fact, he was as much a dilettante in religion as in other things. Suetonius says (*Nero*, 56) that he despised all religious cults. This perhaps applies to traditional Roman religion; Suetonius also refers to his short-lived devotion to a Syrian goddess and subsequently to a good luck charm. The visit of Tiridates in which the

Parthian king addressed Nero as the incarnation of Mithras and used language appropriate to the divine monarchies of the East may have had its effect on the imagination of the emperor but it was probably short-lived. Nero enthusiastically took up the 'religion of the Magi' (as the Parthian system was generally known) and is said to have been initiated into it by Tiridates in person, but he soon gave it up as an illusion when it failed to provide him with the occult and magical powers for which he seems to have hoped.

The Fire of Rome in 64 and its Consequences

THE most sensational event of Nero's principate was the great fire of Rome in 64, and his alleged responsibility for it added an important element to the legend of Nero in later generations. The fire broke out on the night of 18 July in the part of the Circus Maximus nearest to the Palatine and Esquiline hills. The inflammable materials in the shops where it began soon blazed fiercely and a wind fanned the flames through the neighbouring quarters of narrow streets and buildings largely of timber. Of the fourteen regions into which Augustus had divided the city, only I, V, VI, and XIV were entirely undamaged; III, X and XI were completely destroyed and all the other regions suffered damage to a greater or lesser degree. The Forum, the Capitol and part of the Palatine escaped, but there were tremendous losses not only of life and in residential buildings but also in public buildings and temples surviving from early Rome, and of works of art collected from the Greek world.

Nero, who had been at Antium, arrived back in the city when the fire was threatening the *Domus Transitoria* (his palace), which was destroyed. He took energetic measures for the relief of the homeless. Temporary buildings were erected in the Campus Martius and the emperor's own gardens, and he threw open large public buildings. Food was brought in from Ostia and near-by towns and the price of corn was artificially lowered. Demolition was undertaken which halted the fire at the foot of the Esquiline after six days but it broke out again elsewhere and did more damage, though with fewer casualties, for three days more.

According to Tacitus, it was uncertain whether the fire was accidental or had been deliberately started by Nero; all other sources cheerfully attribute the disaster to the emperor. Tacitus will not make a decision, but his own narrative is certainly a combination of two versions, one blaming the emperor, the other stressing his energy in measures of relief. It need hardly be said that the charge of arson has been universally disbelieved by modern scholars. The motives alleged, such as a desire to have room for a new palace, or pure maliciousness, are of the most trivial or *post hoc* sort; the date, a night of full moon in the middle of the Italian summer, was the most unsuitable that could be chosen, and Nero himself was absent at the time. Besides, the fire was only the largest of a number which had occurred in the crowded city—there had been two in the principate of Tiberius—and everyone knew the dangers. That there was some hindrance to the authorities in their attempt to control the blaze is clear but attributable not to the emperor's hirelings but to looters, the inevitable accompaniment of such disasters in ancient as in modern times.

Suetonius says that Nero watched the fire from the Tower of Maecenas and, being moved by the beauty of the flames, sang of the Sack of Troy, dressed in his tragic costume; Dio located this alleged incident on the roof of the palace. Tacitus, much more prudently, states that a rumour ran through the city at the time of the fire itself that the emperor had sung of the Sack of Troy in his private theatre in his gardens. Despite these inconsistencies and the tendentious accounts of the fire as a whole, the image of a ruler 'fiddling while Rome burned' is far too potent, and useful, ever to be discarded from popular imagination.

Immediately after the fire there was superstitious panic as well as rumours hostile to Nero. In the traditional manner of the Romans in such circumstances, the mysterious Sibylline books were consulted to see what rites and ceremonies were needed to appease the gods. But, says Tacitus (*Annals* XV, 44):

> Neither human resources nor the emperor's generosity nor the appeasement of the gods sufficed to quell the suspicion that the fire had been instigated by Nero. To suppress this rumour he fabricated scapegoats and pun-

ished with the most refined tortures those who were popularly called 'Chrestiani', who were hated for their crimes. The originator of this name was Christus who had been executed in the principate of Tiberius by the procurator Pontius Pilate. Although suppressed by this for a while, the pernicious superstition broke out again not only in Judaea, where the evil had begun, but also in the city, where all disgraceful and shameful practices from all over the world collect and flourish. First, those who confessed [i.e. they were 'Chrestiani'] were arrested, and on their information large numbers were convicted not so much for incendiarism as for their hatred of the human race. Their deaths were made objects of amusement; dressed in the skins of wild animals they were torn to pieces by dogs, or crucified or burned alive, being used as torches when daylight ended. Nero provided his gardens for the spectacle and exhibited displays in the Circus mixing with the people dressed as a charioteer or standing on a chariot. As a result, the victims were pitied although guilty and deserving the harshest penalties, on the ground that they were being destroyed to gratify the cruelty of one man rather than for the public good.

This famous passage, the first in a pagan author to mention the origin of Christianity, has been the subject of innumerable commentaries not only because of its intrinsic interest but also because of its difficulties. These really lie not so much in the text itself as in the sequel. No other writer, Christian or pagan, in the following centuries refers to Nero using the Christians as scapegoats, though Christian tradition knew of Nero as a persecutor; Christian hagiography, which liked to dwell on the cruelty of the martyrs' deaths, did not use this sensational example; Christian writers who regularly found it necessary to defend their faith against such charges as incest or cannibalism never mention the charge of setting fire to Rome; the martyrdoms of Peter and Paul were not associated with the fire in the admittedly legendary tradition formed in the third century, and in fact Eusebius, the founder of Christian chronology, dated them to 67–68.

Suetonius (*Nero*, 16) says 'the " Christiani", members of a new and dangerous superstition, were punished' (Christiani and Chrestiani were regular alternative spellings), but does not connect measures against the Christians with the fire. It would, however, be unwise to doubt Tacitus in a matter such as this; besides, burning alive is well attested as the regular penalty for incendiarism, a not infrequent crime in Rome, while exposure to the wild beasts or crucifixion also indicates the non-citizen and slave element which was numerous among the early Christians. While the public, even festive, nature of the occasion testifies to the brutalizing effects of the amphitheatre on generations of Romans, there may also have been a quasi-religious, expiatory character in the punishments; in earlier days, the Romans had once or twice in great crises even felt driven to human sacrifice.

The Christians were not at this stage being 'persecuted' for their religion, though they were undoubtedly unpopular because of it and hence obvious scapegoats. Foreign cults were not forbidden in Rome and Italy, though they had to be approved by the Senate, nor was participation in them forbidden even to Roman citizens, provided that this did not involve desertion of Roman religion. Earlier actions against the devotees of Bacchus in the Republic and of Isis under Tiberius had been taken because these religions were believed to lead to unrest, political disorder or actual crime. Up to this time, no religion within the Empire had adopted an exclusive attitude except Judaism, which was, however, allowed some privileges in this respect. The unique character of Judaism is one of the main reasons why so few Roman citizens became Jews and vice versa; there was a famous case under Nero of the wife of a senator being accused of adopting a foreign superstition, probably Judaism, and its seriousness lay in the desertion of Roman gods which this would entail. In the case of Jews and Christians, social exclusiveness—'hatred of the human race'—went with religion. Such exclusiveness remained for some time a cause of the unpopularity of the new religion.

Furthermore, the religious observances of the Christians were held to be orgiastic and criminal because of some of the words and symbols used. Tacitus seems not to have believed that they were guilty of incendiarism, but to have accepted that they were otherwise criminal and hence justly punished. They were not attacked elsewhere, however, nor were the measures in Rome binding on governors in the provinces. The basis of the persecutions, properly so called, was somewhat different after the death of Nero, when the charge of incendiarism obviously sank into oblivion, and when Christian religious rites were no longer believed to be criminal. No convincing explanation of the silence of later generations about a connexion between the measures against the Christians and the fire of Rome exists. Tacitus' work was more or less forgotten; as for the Christian tradition, it may be supposed that almost the entire Christian community at Rome was destroyed and that later arrivals and converts in the city had no reason to cherish the memory of those who had suffered, particularly as no issue of religious faith was directly involved.

The fire of Rome was followed by an outburst of public building in which Nero surpassed all his predecessors. Even before this date, he had continued the tradition of imperial enterprise in building which dated from Augustus, or rather Julius Caesar, and had Hellenistic precedents. It was characteristic of the energy of Caesar that within his short dictatorship, and with many other concerns, he had formed projects for major works in Italy and the provinces—a new harbour at Ostia, the Tiber below Rome to be diverted into a canal leading to the sea at Terracina, the draining of the Pomptine marshes, and a canal through the isthmus of Corinth. It was equally characteristic of the conservatism of his successors that none of these projects was attempted for nearly a century, and that what was held laudable when planned by Caesar was judged extravagant when undertaken by Nero. Augustus did an enormous amount to give the city of Rome the appearance proper to the capital of the Empire, though much of what he did was to restore and embellish buildings of the past. His immediate successors did less; important aqueducts were begun by Gaius and completed by Claudius, and the latter began at last a new harbour at Ostia. This was probably not completed till well on in Nero's principate; it was in use in 62 and celebrated on the coinage in 64.

At the very beginning of Nero's principate, a temple to the deified Claudius was begun, but was soon suspended when Agrippina's power waned—it was completed by Vespasian. A triumphal arch to commemorate the victories of Corbulo is mentioned in both the sources and on the coinage. More important was the *Macellum Magnum* (Great Market) on the Caelian, dedicated in 56–57. A large circular building of two stories, it is represented on coins in the later years of Nero's principate, a fact which probably indicates its popularity in Rome. In connexion with his enthusiasm for games on the Greek model, he built and dedicated in 61 or 62 a gymnasium. It suffered from fire the same year, but apparently was not destroyed. Associated with it were the *Thermae Neronianae* (Nero's Baths), only the second public bathing establishment in Rome. The group of buildings was one of the most notable in the city and an extremely popular meeting place. Martial wrote (II, 48), 'What was worse than Nero? What is better than Nero's Baths?' They were rebuilt early in the third century by Alexander Severus but enough of the Neronian structure remains to confirm the record in the sources of their splendour and luxury. The Circus Maximus was rebuilt after the fire of 64, and a branch was added to the Aqua Claudia.

It was the great fire that gave Nero the opportunity for his most lavish projects, both private and public. On the one hand, there was a palace to outdo anything undertaken by his predecessors, on the other, a plan to rebuild the destroyed part of the city in a manner which would be both safer and more distinguished than before. In the earlier part of his principate he had already built an extension to the palace of Tiberius and Gaius which he called the *Domus Transitoria*; it was burned in the fire, but evidence survives of its sumptuous use of marble and extensive wall-paintings as decoration. The new palace which he began in 64 astonished contemporaries and can best be described in the words of Suetonius (*Nero*, 31):

> There was nothing in which Nero was more prodigal than in his buildings. He built a palace extending from the Palatine to the Esquiline Hill which he first called the *Domus Transitoria* but, when it was burned down shortly after completion and rebuilt, the *Domus Aurea* [Golden House]. Its size and splendour will be sufficiently indicated by the following details. The vestibule was so large that it could contain a colossal statue of the emperor 120 feet high and it was so extensive that it had a triple portico a mile long. There was a lake like the sea, surrounded by buildings to look like cities, besides tracts of country, cornfields, vineyards, pastures and woods, with great numbers of wild and domestic animals. In the rest of the palace, everything was overlaid with gold and ornamented with gems and mother of pearl. The dining rooms were panelled and had ivory ceilings whose panels could turn and shower down flowers; and pipes to sprinkle perfumes. The main banqueting hall was circular and constantly revolved day and night like the heavens. He had baths supplied with sea water and sulphur water. When he had dedicated the completed palace he said nothing more by way of approval than that at last he was beginning to be housed like a human being.

A number of the rooms of the Esquiline wing of the Golden House are embedded in the cellars of the Baths of Trajan which subsequently occupied the site, but they were not the main rooms of the palace. All are of concrete construction and vaulted. There are remains of wall-paintings, perhaps those of the painter Famulus praised by the elder Pliny. The importance of the building in the history of architecture is considerable. It realized for the first time on a large scale an understanding of the artistic uses of the vault, and was very different from the rectangular plan and flat roofs of the traditional Roman building. The variety which could now be attained was enormous. Again, it imported into the city the 'improvements on Nature' characteristic of the great villas of the country and the seaside—the park, the lake, pavilions and so on. The setting described by Suetonius is similar to that represented on a number of wall-paintings from Pompeii. The whole conception was thoroughly in tune with Nero's love of the marvellous, his enthusiasm for the arts, his rejection of Roman conventions and his desire to appear in an unrivalled setting. The mechanical devices in the ceilings are confirmed by Seneca who knew of others, probably in the *Domus Transitoria*, with movable parts which could be changed to present a different pattern at each course at dinner.

In spite of what Suetonius says, the palace was never completed. Otho advanced the work, but Vitellius disliked it and his wife ridiculed the decorations, presumably because of their advanced taste. It is generally assumed that the whole thing was thoroughly unpopular, though it is not certain that this was so; there is a reluctant admiration of it in the sources, perhaps derived ultimately from the elder Pliny. Nevertheless, there was resentment that it covered such a large part of the city, and the cost was enormous; as Tacitus put it (*Annals* XV, 42), the architects Severus and Celer 'had the genius and the courage to attempt by their skill what was against the decrees of Nature, and to fritter away the resources of an emperor'. Vespasian prudently turned most of the buildings and the park to public use, and the Colosseum (Flavian Amphitheatre) which he built within its precincts was far more suited to Roman taste than the elegance of the palace and its surroundings.

A major attempt was made to replan the destroyed parts of the city and to enforce new building regulations. Tacitus is very favourable to Nero's efforts (*Annals* XV, 43):

In the parts of Rome not occupied by the [new] Palace, rebuilding was not indiscriminate and unplanned as after the burning of the city by the Gauls [390 B.C.]. The streets were of regulated dimensions and alignments, and were of substantial width, the height of houses was restricted, there were open spaces and the frontages of the blocks were protected by colonnades. Nero undertook to build these colonnades at his own expense and to clear débris from building sites before handing them over to their owners. He announced rewards proportionate to rank and property to those who completed new houses or blocks before a given date. Débris was to be dumped in the Ostian marshes by corn ships returning down the Tiber. A fixed proportion of all buildings was to be of solid untimbered structure of Gabine or Alban stone which is fireproof. Further, there were to be guards to insure that the water supply which had been intercepted by private lawlessness should be available for the public in greater quantities and at more points. Householders were to keep fire fighting apparatus in an accessible place. There were to be no joint partitions between buildings—each was to have its separate wall. These reforms were welcome for their utility and added to the beauty of the new city.

The extent to which all this was carried through in the four remaining years of Nero's principate is not known. In the end, the planned rebuilding was certainly never completed, no doubt for reasons similar to the failure in London after the Great Fire in 1666—and for that matter more recent times. However, it was not without its effect in towns and cities of Italy where it can be seen in Ostia.

As mentioned above, Claudius had built a new port at Ostia which was certainly in use by 62. Whether or not it had been intended to receive the Egyptian corn fleet, in fact it was not so used, though it must have had some beneficial effects on the food situation at Rome. The importance attached to this since the late Republic needs no description here; it was summed up in the famous gibe that the Roman poor cared for nothing except 'bread and circuses'. Outbreaks of violence at times of shortage were a constant fear of the emperors; Claudius is said to have been chased from the Forum by an angry mob on one occasion. Yet it was probably he who rationalized the distribution of cheap corn at Rome (over 200,000 people enjoyed the benefit) under a freedman subordinate to the *praefectus annonae* (prefect of the corn supply). Nero was equally concerned. In 58 some of the regulations to curb the *publicani* also made the movement of corn supplies in the provinces easier, and at the same time it was ruled that ship-owners should not pay property-tax on their ships. In 62 he ordered mildewed stocks to be thrown into the Tiber, and it is implied that this was to inspire the people with confidence that there was plenty of good corn left. In the same year, 200 corn ships were wrecked at Ostia and 100 burnt in the Tiber without causing a rise in prices.

The disaster at Ostia (and many ships of the fleet were also wrecked off Cumae in 64) showed the danger of the west coast of the Italian peninsula. When the corn ships put in at Puteoli their cargo still had to be transhipped up the coast to Ostia. It was these considerations which had led Julius Caesar to plan a canal from the lower Tiber to Terracina in order to reduce the length of the coastal journey. Nero went further and planned a canal to run from Ostia to Lake Avernus. At the latter end this would have involved the rebuilding of the Portus Julius built by Agrippa in 37 B.C. when he joined Lake Avernus with Lake Lucrinus and made a navigable exit to the sea. The length of the canal would have been about 135 Roman (125 English) miles and it was to be wide enough for quinqueremes to pass each other. An incidental benefit would have been the draining of the Pomptine marshes. The scheme was to be completed by a canal from Ostia into the city of Rome to avoid the bends and rapids of the Tiber. Nero also planned to extend Rome's city walls to Ostia—an idea surely modelled on the Long Walls linking ancient Athens with her port at Piraeus. The team of Severus and Celer, who had built the Golden House, was responsible for the scheme, which seems to have been begun before 64. Convict labour from all over the Empire was to be used—it was said that no other sentences except hard labour on the canal were allowed. It was in connexion with the attempt to pierce the hills near Avernus that Tacitus (*Annals* XV, 42) called Nero a 'lover of the incredible'. Like the Corinth canal, the project was abandoned at his death, and Tacitus may have been justified in complaining that the anticipated advantages did not justify the labour. We do not hear of many difficulties with corn supplies in the following years, and the growing exports from Africa, together with Trajan's vast new work at Ostia early in the second century, provided still greater security for the food supplies.

A canal through the isthmus of Corinth had been projected before Nero by a Hellenistic king, Demetrius, and later by Julius Caesar and Gaius. The plans of the latter may have been in existence for Nero to use, since the work seems to have got under way with great speed. It was inaugurated during 67 by Nero in person; 6,000 Jewish captives were sent by Vespasian and praetorian soldiers also took part, presumably in a supervisory capacity. A number of shafts and trenches from Nero's scheme were visible when the modern canal was built on the identical line in the nineteenth century. The economic advantages to Greece in ancient conditions are problematical, but were believed to be considerable; the rounding of the Peloponnese past Cape Malea was a notorious hazard. Critics were not lacking, but some gave credit to the emperor for showing 'a spirit even better than Greek' in his enterprise.

Nevertheless, all Nero's great projects remained unfinished. Common sense dictated the abandonment of the Golden House, while private property rights no doubt triumphed over the replanning of the city. As for the canals, we cannot be certain why they were never resumed by later emperors. Cost was no doubt one reason; the resources of the emperor were not unlimited and he was no Pharaoh who could treat all his subjects as slaves. The roads, aqueducts and harbours of the Empire show that the Romans had a proper estimate of practical utility, and they may have correctly decided that Nero's (and Caesar's) canals were not worth the effort. Revulsion against Nero's megalomania also played its part. It seems likely that he was going to rename the Peloponnesus (Island of Pelops) Neronesus when the canal was completed, and he may even have gone so far as to think of renaming the city of Rome after himself.

The Conspiracy of Piso, 65

THE execution by Claudius of many senators and knights had been bitterly resented. Some were no doubt implicated in the revolt of Camillus Scribonianus in 42, and some in Messalina's scheme, whatever it actually was. The remainder were victims of the tension between the emperor and the two orders as he and his household freedmen exercised more direct control over the administration of the Empire. For the first eight years of Nero's principate there had been no such victims. Those who had been sacrificed to the emperor's resentments or suspicions had all been members or connexions of the imperial family, always its own worst enemy. Most are represented as innocent of anything except being a potential threat to the emperor's security, but in the judgement of the time such victims were not in the same category as other senators, and their deaths did not arouse the violent hostility of the Senate.

The law of *maiestas* (treason) was revived in 62 for the first time since the death of Claudius. The accused was the praetor Antistius Sosianus, who composed some scurrilous verses about Nero and recited them at a party. Since the time of Augustus such attacks on the emperor could be regarded as treasonable. Antistius was prosecuted before the Senate and found guilty; the consul designate proposed the sentence of death by scourging. Thrasea Paetus opposed this on the ground that such a penalty was obsolete for senators, and proposed exile instead. The senators, who had at first favoured the death penalty, swung over to Thrasea's view and it was approved by a large majority. The consuls were afraid formally to accept the vote, and informed Nero. The emperor wrote back saying that he would anyway have mitigated the harsher sentence and agreeing to abide by any decision taken, even an acquittal. Thrasea and the majority stood firm and Antistius was exiled. Tacitus said that Nero was angry, but this is not confirmed by his paraphrase of the letter, and it is probable that Nero would have vetoed the death penalty; when it came to actual plotters later, none (of high rank, at any rate) suffered death by scourging, and most were permitted to commit suicide. Perhaps the initial feeling in favour of scourging resulted from fear that Antistius' insults would infuriate Nero against the whole Senate.

The condemnation of Antistius occurred in the same year as the death of Burrus and the retirement of Seneca, which Tacitus regarded as a turning point in Nero's principate. However, he fails to prove any immediate deterioration in relations with the Senate. It is true that the record of senatorial debates, trials of governors and other political matters in Rome and Italy and the provinces, which he chronicled under each year, comes almost to a stop in 62. If this is not due to his sources, it may indicate that Nero's new advisers were less conscientious than Seneca and his friends, but hardly that they were at odds with the Senate. Those whose names we know (besides Tigellinus), such as Cluvius Rufus the historian, Vestinus Atticus, consul in 65 and a man of outspoken character, the future emperor Vespasian, and C. Petronius, also of consular rank and famous as Nero's model in matters of taste, were all men of standing and experience. Thus, though dissatisfaction with Nero was growing, a crisis in relations with the Senate was deferred till the discovery of a major conspiracy in 65.

The object of the conspiracy was the assassination of Nero and his replacement as emperor by the noble C. Calpurnius Piso, though he was not its originator. A member of one of the surviving Republican families, he had had to surrender his first wife to Gaius, who exiled him. Recalled by Claudius, he had obtained a suffect consulship and some governorships but not an important military command. He was popular with the people because of his generosity and affability, and he did not parade a forbidding morality. He was a literary patron and a poet himself and had appeared on the stage, presumably in Nero's Juvenalia or the Neronia; this did not endear him to the stricter element.

The motives of the conspirators were various, some quite trivial; Lucan is said to have joined because he had been forbidden to publish, Afranius Quintianus because he had been insulted in a lampoon by Nero, Faenius Rufus because he feared the influence of his co-prefect Tigellinus. The consul designate Plautius Lateranus and the courageous freedwoman Epicharis were moved by *amor reipublicae* (patriotism, whatever this implied). The participation of Faenius Rufus, with three tribunes and three centurions of the praetorian guard, had a double significance. No conspiracy had much chance of success without the support of the praetorians; more important, officers of the guard were naturally chosen for reliability as well as efficiency; they came from Italian towns whose upper classes had a tradition of loyal service to the emperors and where senatorial pretensions were little regarded. Tacitus attests the actual words of the tribune Subrius Flavus (one of the most active of the conspirators) when asked by Nero why he had broken his oath: 'I hated you, though no soldier was more loyal when you deserved our love. I began to hate you when you became the murderer of your mother and wife, a charioteer, an actor and an incendiary.' Disgust at the crimes of Nero, and still more at his degradation of the authority of the imperial position, undoubtedly inspired the majority of the active conspirators.

The plot came to a head in April 65. The freedwoman Epicharis tried to win over the prefect of the fleet at Misenum, who disclosed the plot to Nero. Epicharis had given no details and there were no witnesses, but she was detained. The conspirators now had to hurry. A proposal to kill Nero at Piso's villa at Baiae was rejected since Piso feared that someone else would be proclaimed emperor at Rome when the news was out; there was L. Silanus, last of the descendants of Augustus, and the consul Vestinus Atticus, who was believed to have Republican sympathies but also to be capable of furthering some other claimant. The assassination was then planned to take place at Rome during games in the Circus; Piso was to wait near by and when Nero was dead would be taken to the praetorian camp by Faenius Rufus along with (it was said) Claudius' daughter Antonia.

The plot was revealed the day before it matured when a senatorial conspirator named Scaevinus aroused the suspicions of one of his freedmen, who rushed to inform Nero. Scaevinus and an associate Natalis were arrested, and under threat of torture revealed what they knew. Natalis implicated Piso and accused Seneca, while Scaevinus named Lucan, Afranius Quintianus and Claudius Senecio, earlier one of Nero's closest friends. Lucan in turn is said to have implicated his mother, and Senecio his friend Annius Pollio. In contrast, the freedwoman Epicharis endured a day's torture (not known to have been applied to any of the others) and revealed nothing; she committed suicide the next day before further interrogation.

As Nero doubled his bodyguard and sent troops to arrest suspects and bring them before him, the conspiracy collapsed. Faenius Rufus, who had not yet been denounced, sought to escape by the vigour of his interrogation of suspects. Some urged Piso to appeal to the troops and the people rather than supinely wait his inevitable end but he refused. He was allowed to commit suicide. In contrast, Plautius Lateranus was executed by one of the tribunes in the plot. The next victim was Seneca. It is not clear whether or not he knew of the conspiracy; there was a story which said that Subrius Flavus and the centurions in the plot intended to remove Piso after they had killed Nero and make Seneca emperor; Tacitus does not vouch for it. Seneca, who had approved in his works the Stoic doctrines of suicide, received the order to die with fortitude. Subsequently Faenius Rufus and the military members of the conspiracy were denounced and executed with one exception who, however, committed suicide after acquittal. Nero had expected the implication of the consul Vestinus in the plot but this was not forthcoming. They had at one time been friends and Nero is said to have experienced the reckless and savage wit of Vestinus. He was ordered to commit suicide. This was followed by the suicide of Lucan and other leading conspirators.

In most of these cases Tacitus related the brief circumstances of the deaths and last words and actions of the condemned on the basis of accounts written in his own lifetime, which recorded the deaths of Nero's victims. The scenes were generally similar. The victims received the order to die from an officer sent by Nero; after setting their affairs in order and saying farewell to their families and friends they committed suicide by opening the arteries in the arm, concerned to display true Roman, or Stoic, fortitude. The literary genre which recorded their last hours really approximated to later Christian martyr literature, though its object was to commemorate not a religious faith but the courage of Roman gentlemen at the mercy of a tyrant. In the conspiracy and its immediate aftermath there were nineteen deaths and thirteen exiles; among the latter some were regarded by Tacitus as innocent.

Nero ordered a large donative to be given to the soldiers. At a meeting of the Senate he had triumphal insignia bestowed on Petronius Turpilianus, Cocceius Nerva (the future emperor) and Tigellinus, no doubt for services rendered in the crisis. Consular insignia were given to Nymphidius Sabinus who replaced Faenius Rufus as praetorian prefect. Various adulatory votes were passed, including one to rename the month of April after the emperor.

The suppression of the conspiracy brought little security to Nero. He may have had nothing to fear from within the imperial family as it had been reduced in the intrigues of the previous decades to a mere handful of obscure members, but this only increased the possibility of further conspiracies like that of Piso. Nero badly wanted children if only for reasons of the succession but was disappointed. In 63 Poppaea had given him a daughter, Claudia, but the baby died after three months.

In 65, some time after the conspiracy, came another disaster, the death of Poppaea. It was said that Nero was personally responsible, since he had kicked her in a temper while she was pregnant. Full of remorse, he had her deified. The following year he tried unsuccessfully to strengthen his dynastic position by proposing marriage to Antonia, surviving daughter of Claudius. It was hardly surprising that she refused in view of the fate of her father, her half-sister and her husband Faustus Sulla. As a result of her refusal, Nero had her executed on a charge of conspiracy though Tacitus had his doubts whether she was guilty. Subsequently Nero married Statilia Messalina, rich, beautiful and clever. The marriage allied Nero to a family powerful since the time of Augustus; Nero was her fifth husband—the fourth had been Vestinus Atticus, executed the previous year.

Meanwhile, after the death of Poppaea, and because he was now aware of the hostility with which he was viewed by much of the Senate, Nero denounced in person or accepted charges against a series of prominent men, in almost all cases on trivial grounds. It should be noted that in most cases, as under other emperors, formal trials were held, and Tacitus has often been accused of ignoring or even misrepresenting the formal charges and the speeches of the prosecution and the defence. There is something in this but the reason is clear; in treason trials under an autocratic régime, legal process is a mere formality; what matters is the penalty. Firstly the elderly jurist C. Cassius Longinus was forbidden to attend the funeral of Poppaea, a renunciation of friendship such as Nero had directed against Thrasea Paetus in 63. Nero also denounced Cassius' nephew L. Silanus and asked the Senate to exile both. Cassius was said to have preserved among his ancestral portraits one of Cassius (the assassin of Caesar) which bore the inscription 'Leader of the Party', and to have brought forward his nephew as a potential revolutionary. The latter was also suspect as a descendant of Augustus; another uncle, D. Silanus Torquatus, had been accused of treason in 64 and committed suicide. Cassius and L. Silanus were both exiled;

Cassius survived till the principate of Vespasian, but Silanus was soon killed. Next fell L. Antistius Vetus, who had held the consulship with Nero in 55, his mother-in-law Sextia and his daughter Pollitta, presumably because their hatred of Nero was assumed—Pollitta was the widow of Rubellius Plautus.

In 66 better grounds were alleged against the consular P. Anteius and Ostorius Scapula, son of the former governor of Britain; they had both consulted an astrologer about their own fate and that of the emperor, a capital offence; they committed suicide before trial. This was followed by the deaths of Rufrius Crispinus, former praetorian prefect who had been exiled the previous year; the brother of Seneca and father of Lucan, Annaeus Mela, who was now accused of complicity in the conspiracy (Seneca's other brother Gallio was also forced to commit suicide this year); Anicius Cerealis, one of the consuls of 65, and Petronius, whose life of eccentric refinement had been so admired by Nero that he became the emperor's model in matters of taste. Finally in this year Nero attacked 'virtue itself', as Tacitus has it, in the persons of Thrasea Paetus and Barea Soranus. In the case of the former, his Stoic views were important, and the affair is central to an estimate of the place which Stoicism had in the opposition to Nero during his final years.

Stoicism and the Opposition to Nero

STOICISM had long been the most influential of Greek philosophical schools in Rome. The emphasis in its ethic on private and public duties, on doing with fortitude what had to be done, its austere, even puritanical streak, and increasingly its claim to give calm and strength to the will in the face of the harsh realities of life, appealed to much in the Roman tradition. In an age when standards of conduct had lost their traditional basis, and to those who could believe in neither the old gods nor the new, it was undoubtedly a support. In its political influence under the Empire, however, there is a paradox. Traditional Stoicism had taught the superiority of a so-called mixed constitution, a blend of monarchy, aristocracy and democracy, but the school in general was sympathetic to the idea of monarchy as the most 'natural' and therefore the 'best' form of government. Seneca repeated this view on a number of occasions, as did his younger contemporary Musonius Rufus, who could certainly not be accused of accommodating his views to political necessity. It is true that the theory insisted that the monarchy should be a just one; as Seneca said (*De Beneficiis* II, 20), 'the best condition of the state is under a just king'. But there was no consistent tradition of resistance to rulers who fell short of the ideal among Stoics or for that matter among Cynics who, although critical of all institutions, generally accepted the theory of monarchy. There was nothing in Stoicism as such which should have led to the accusation that Stoics were trouble makers.

Philosophy could be regarded as escapist, and certainly the view that philosophy was a useless pursuit was traditional in Rome and still held in Nero's lifetime. Agrippina had diverted Nero from the subject as unsuitable for a future emperor, and in 58 Seneca's enemy

P. Suillius had contrasted his own practice of eloquence in the turmoil of the lawcourts with Seneca's useless intellectual pursuits. There was also the example of Tacitus' father-in-law Agricola (see above, p. 26), and the historian praised Helvidius Priscus for his approach to philosophy which was not 'as in most cases in order to conceal indolence under a high sounding name but in order to take part in politics fortified against its changes of fortune'. It could in fact be argued that a Stoic should not take part in political life since such activity was bound to cause him anxiety and stress and be an obstacle to the achievement of inner peace. Thus Seneca said, 'If the state is too corrupt to be improved, if it is entirely overwhelmed by evil, the philosopher should not strive in vain' (*De Otio* III, 3); he could criticize the Stoic hero Cato for taking part in the struggles which ended the Republic, since the destruction of liberty was inevitable. However, the argument for inactivity was outweighed by the Stoic precept that a man must play his part in the sphere of life in which Providence had placed him, and this coincided with the traditional obligations of the Roman senator.

The view of Nero and his associates is expressed most clearly in the account of Tigellinus' attack on Rubellius Plautus in 62: 'He does not even pretend to like retirement but parades his admiration of the ancient Romans and has also adopted the arrogance of the Stoics, a sect which makes men turbulent and eager for political activity' (Tacitus, *Annals* XIV, 57). Making eagerness for political activity a ground for an accusation was a total reversal of normal Roman values, and no doubt Tacitus wanted his readers so to take it, as an indication of the climate of Nero's principate. The idea appeared again when Thrasea Paetus was compared by his accusers not only with Cato, the enemy of Caesar, but with two notorious Stoics of the Republic, Aelius Tubero and M. Favonius, whose characteristic was held to be meddling in affairs which did not concern them. Seneca felt bound to rebut the charge, as shown in the quotation overleaf.

In my view, it is a mistake to believe that those who have loyally devoted themselves to philosophy are stubborn and rebellious, scorners of magistrates or kings or others who control the state. On the contrary, no one is more popular with the philosopher than the ruler, and rightly, because the ruler bestows on none a greater privilege than upon those who are allowed to enjoy peace and leisure. Hence those who profit by the safety provided by the state in their pursuit of virtuous living must cherish as a father the author of this good, at any rate much more than those restless persons who are at the centre of affairs, who owe much to the ruler but expect much from him and are never so liberally rewarded that their desires, growing from being supplied, are entirely satisfied (*Epistles* 73).

This, however, clearly evaded the charge that philosophers in public as opposed to private life were dangerous.

There was another objection, at first sight superficial but undoubtedly widespread. The virtues of the austere and simple life had always been one of the essentials of both Stoic and Cynic teaching. The examples of Socrates and other individuals had encouraged the growth of a recognizable appearance and a way of life for the philosopher. He was expected to be plain to the point of eccentricity in his dress, wear a long beard and possess a severity of appearance to match his austere doctrines. 'They are full of empty boasting, and if one of them grows a long beard and elevates his eyebrows, and throws his cloak over his shoulder and goes barefoot, he claims immediately to have wisdom, courage and righteousness . . . they despise everyone and call the man of good family effeminate, the low-born poor-spirited, the handsome man a debauchee, the ugly simple-minded, the rich covetous and the poor greedy.'

Thus Vespasian's friend Mucianus on the Stoics and Cynics about 75, according to Dio (LXVI, 13). Many Romans were as irritated by claims to superior virtue as people in modern societies; the austere appearance of Thrasea Paetus—'like a schoolmaster', according to

Suetonius (*Nero*, 37)—and that of his associates was held to be a deliberate reproach to Nero's whole way of life, and there is little doubt that there was truth in this.

In view of the ambiguities of the Stoic position, it is not surprising that some historians have minimized its importance in the opposition to Nero, and argued that it merely provided a rationalization of the prejudices of the Roman upper class, a veneer of high morality for narrow political aims. It is a fact that most of the known Stoics who figured in opposition to emperors were senators, and a number were connected by family ties. Some of their careers were distinguished, and there is evidence that their opposition was inspired at least in part by a limited concept of senatorial liberty —in practice, freedom to express views in the Senate and to deliver a corporate opinion without fear and without the necessity of displaying servile adulation of the ruler. There is also an assumption that Roman politicians of every age were realists who invariably acted in terms of a crude assessment of personal or family advantage, and that their only ideas, if such they could be called, were those of the traditional Roman ethic, in terms of which Roman politicians acted and were judged by their peers.

However, the crisis of Nero's principate was far more than the dissatisfaction of a few disgruntled senators. There was a great difference between the circumstances of the successful nobility of the second and first centuries B.C. and the Senate of the later Julio-Claudians, insecure and humiliated by the emperor. The *mos maiorum* (traditional code) was not merely for private life but assumed, for the rich, a life of public activity and political competition. But under the emperors, political activity was restricted, and the *mos maiorum* seemed accordingly to be out of touch with reality. No doubt the great majority were relatively untroubled and solved the dilemma, if they felt it, in a pragmatic way; the Roman Empire existed and must be served, loyal service to the emperor could be equated with service to the Roman state; one would pray for good emperors but put up with bad ones. But a number of thoughtful men found this impossible in the face of some of the features of Nero's principate.

The potentialities of Stoicism as a focus of resistance were increased by its association with Cato. The myth of Cato was an extraordinary phenomenon; the fact that it sprang into being almost immediately after his death in 46 B.C. testifies to his own moral ascendancy (often underestimated by modern historians) and to the intensity of the emotions caused by the fall of the Republic and the dictatorship of Julius Caesar. That earlier crisis produced its needed hero in the Roman noble who was also a Stoic and who committed suicide rather than survive the death of the Republic. Cato came to represent the loss of liberty—a liberty which was not easy to define, and which realists might associate with no more than the licence of aristocratic politicians, but which was conspicuously absent in the principate. A similar but lesser devotion attached to the tyrannicides Brutus and Cassius, whose non-Stoic views were quietly forgotten. Public display of their images was forbidden by Augustus and Tiberius; under the latter there was a famous case in which the historian Cremutius Cordus was accused of praising Brutus and calling Cassius 'last of the Romans'; his books were burned and he committed suicide. In the prosecution of Thrasea Paetus, Cossutianus Capito suggested that whereas once the Roman state had had Caesar and Cato as its two rivals, now it was Nero and Thrasea.

The fact that the brief hopes of a restored Republic at the end of Gaius' principate had only lasted a day does not mean that they could not revive in the minds of a few in the next generation—Vestinus Atticus for example. Not everyone had the total pessimism of Tacitus, and there was still more disillusionment to go through under the Flavians before there was a final reconciliation between philosophy and the principate. However, it was doubtless the case that most Stoics would hope for a just ruler rather than a problematical return to Republican government, and if the Cynics were more extreme, it must be observed that the only known members of the School at this time, Demetrius and Isidorus, were Greeks. This does not mean that it was Nero's crimes and frivolities alone which produced the major crisis of opinion; it was the phenomenon of *adulatio*, the servility with which the worst imperial crimes must be congratulated, which was so offensive. As has been said, 'When many of the rights usually connected with Roman *libertas* were lost, some people rediscovered what the Greek philosophers had noticed before, that loss of political rights involves almost un-expectedly a much more serious offence to elementary moral values.'[1]

The evils of *adulatio* were a major concern of Tacitus. There can be no doubt that he personally felt guilt for his own participation in such scenes in the principate of Domitian, and expressed it not ignobly in his *Agricola*. In the extended historical work, *adulatio* is part of the demoralization of society brought about by the emperors; it resulted from the fact that there was no effective check on imperial despotism. The emperor's subjects were concerned at best for their own survival, at worst to gain advantage from the tyrant's behaviour. In the Neronian books, Tacitus says, after recording the murder of Octavia (*Annals* XIV, 64),

> How long shall I continue to record the thank-offerings in the temples on such occasions? Every reader of that period of history in my own works or the works of others can assume that the gods were thanked every time the emperor ordered a banishment or murder, and that what were formerly the accompaniments of national success be-came the marks of public disasters. Nevertheless, when any decree of the Senate reaches new depths of adulation or servility I will not leave it unrecorded.

Senators were in a position in which they must act in a way offensive on grounds of both personal and

[1] A. Momigliano, *Journal of Roman Studies*, Vol. XLI (1951), p. 148.

public morality, or risk exile or death; moral and political objections to Nero were in fact inseparable. Stoic doctrines were entirely relevant to this situation, and it is not surprising that Stoic teachings about facing death, and still more about the ethic of suicide in intolerable circumstances, were emphasized by the Roman Stoics in response. The actions of Thrasea Paetus should be looked at in the light of these considerations.

Thrasea was a 'new man' from Padua and was consul in 56; he was an assiduous senator, and became very influential early in Nero's principate. He was accustomed to pass over in silence or with brief assent senatorial motions of an adulatory kind, and in 59 he walked out of the Senate House when thanksgiving decrees were being passed on Nero's 'escape' from Agrippina. This hazardous action is said to have brought no increase in senatorial liberty; but three years later it was precisely Thrasea's leadership which gave the Senate the strength not to condemn Antistius Sosianus to death. In the same year he secured a decree on the subject of congratulatory votes to provincial governors. In 63, however, he was forbidden by Nero to come with the rest of the Senate to Antium on the birth of Claudia. Subsequently Thrasea abstained entirely from public life for three years. This was at least in part a deliberate act of disapproval and an attempt to dissociate himself from the régime; when he was finally prosecuted in 66 his accusers represented his withdrawal from public life as treasonable. Thrasea's course of action went as far as anyone could in disapproval, and so far as is known had only been adopted by one other senator, early in the principate of Tiberius.

Thrasea has been described as acting as a courageous and upright Roman senator who held Stoic views, not as a Stoic philosopher who happened to be a senator at Rome. There is truth in this, but his Stoicism should not be underestimated. His assiduous behaviour as a senator, his dislike of adulatory decrees and his attempts to get the Senate to act with some independence are in accordance with the Stoic view of obligations to one's social position; his withdrawal can be interpreted not only as a courageous gesture of protest but also understood in terms of Seneca's view that the Stoic should not strive in vain in a situation beyond redemption. He wrote a life of Cato, and celebrated the birthdays of Brutus and Cassius; he associated with Musonius Rufus, the most elevated mind among Roman Stoics, and with Demetrius the Cynic, and was the friend, if not a patron, of the young satirist and convinced Stoic, Persius.

If we may trust the record of his last hours, he consciously modelled his behaviour on that of Socrates and Cato; he discussed the immortality of the soul with Demetrius, and when he received from a quaestor the senatorial decree of condemnation opened his veins and said, 'I pour a libation to Jupiter the Liberator; look, young man; may the gods avert the omen, but you have been born in an age when examples of fortitude may be useful support' (*Annals* XVI, 35). Thrasea's hope that he would be an example was realized. His biography was written by his friend, the Stoic Junius Arulenus Rusticus, who as a tribune of the plebs in 66 had wanted to veto the Senate's trial but had been prevented by Thrasea from making a useless sacrifice. However, his biographies of Thrasea and of Thrasea's son-in-law Helvidius Priscus brought him the death penalty under Domitian. Helvidius, a convinced Stoic, was exiled because of his relationship to Thrasea and subsequently fell out with Vespasian as well and was executed. Both entered the canon of Stoic 'martyrs' along with Cato and Brutus who were so much admired by the philosopher-emperor Marcus Aurelius.

Much less is known about Barea Soranus and the handful of other Stoic victims. Soranus, who was prosecuted at the same time as Thrasea, was an elderly consular. His Stoic views are known from his friendship with Rubellius Plautus, his association with Thrasea and the fact that he was the patron of Egnatius Celer, a Stoic philosopher, who betrayed his philosophy by prosecuting Soranus. Nothing specific on this score was charged, however; it was alleged that Soranus had hindered Nero's agents in collecting the art treasures of Pergamum when proconsul of Asia and had prepared the province for revolt; besides, his daughter was the wife of Annius Pollio, recently exiled for alleged complicity in the Pisonian conspiracy, and she had imprudently consulted soothsayers about her likely fate. For this, she and her father were required to commit suicide. Also connected with this group was the prosecution of the senator Paconius Agrippinus, a Stoic; no real grounds were given, and he was exiled. Curtius Montanus, a young senator, was accused, it appears, of writing hostile satires; he seems to have been associated with the foregoing victims and was excluded from public life.

It was under Vespasian and again under Domitian that there were mass expulsions of philosophers (specifically, teachers of philosophy) from Rome. No such general measure is attested for Nero's principate, but we know of several individual expulsions (quite apart from the senators mentioned); these included Demetrius the Cynic and Annaeus Cornutus, a Stoic writer of books on rhetoric as well as on philosophy. Musonius Rufus was exiled after the Pisonian conspiracy; probably he was already suspect because of his earlier friendship with Rubellius Plautus, but his exile is associated with that of Verginius Flavus, a prominent rhetorician. Both were influential teachers, and it may be that their influence on their pupils was feared.

In sum, the whole climate of the intellectual and literary world of the Neronian age, with some exceptions such as Petronius and the emperor's own circle, was dominated by Stoicism, and the philosophy became the principal intellectual and moral force of the time. It is not a question of certain authors being influenced by Stoicism; to say this of any Roman writer is no contribution to knowledge. What we have is a number of writers who by education, personal friendships and expressed views can be said to have been convinced Stoics. Nor should it be found surprising if the attitudes of these writers showed differences of emphasis; Stoicism was an adaptable creed and, though it tried, it naturally failed to suppress personality differences.

As has been suggested, we can never fully grasp the personality of Seneca, particularly as a political figure. Much of his surviving work can be dated from the period of his retirement, but there is little to indicate how he justified his career to others, or to himself. His happiness in his retirement seems genuine, and he rarely indulged in sentiments about the folly of ambition and so on. We see him chiefly through the *Epistulae*, a collection of short essays on many topics, primarily philosophical and ethical. In these he approached nearer to Stoic orthodoxy than in his early years. There can be no doubt that for him the problems of personal conduct were, or had now become, paramount. Couched in the form of letters to a friend, the *Epistulae* have a great deal of human appeal. The extreme paradoxes of the Stoic ideal were avoided, and the claims of humanity advanced. Modern critics inevitably seek his comments on such demoralizing features of antiquity as slavery and gladiatorial combats; he was one of the few to be disgusted by the latter, and was in line with Stoic cosmopolitanism in his insistence on treating slaves as human beings, but he inevitably took the institution itself for granted. Elsewhere humanity and common sense combine. For Seneca, the pursuit of virtue was not easy, and earnest study of Stoic principles an essential. Philosophy, moreover, besides being a guide for life was productive of happiness in so far as it fortified the will to accept misfortunes pre-ordained by fate. Stoic doctrine taught men how to face death. Seneca returned to this theme on a number of occasions, and in the end died in accordance with its teachings. It might be supposed that his insistence on this aspect of Stoicism reflected his own fears, but it appears in all contemporaries for the reasons advanced above.

Likewise concerned above all with private as distinct from public concerns was Musonius Rufus, a man of equestrian rank from Volsinii in Etruria. Born about 20, he first appears as a friend of Rubellius Plautus in 62; he was exiled in 65, returned to Rome after the death of Nero, and was active in Rome in 69. Exiled again by

Vespasian he was recalled by Titus and seems to have died before the end of the century. Musonius was the only Roman philosopher to obtain a substantial reputation among Greek thinkers; this was a tribute not only to his personality but also to his acceptance of a much more complete Stoicism than, for example, Seneca, whose unsystematized views could never appeal to the Greeks. Musonius taught in a deliberately Socratic manner, and accordingly all that we know of him is from the accounts of others. He was unquestionably important as a teacher among both Romans in the city (at least till 65) and Greeks, though we know chiefly of the latter; among them were notable figures of the next generation, the most famous being Epictetus. His one known action in politics was unorthodox. In 69 the Flavian forces were at the gates of Rome, there seemed likely to be fighting through the city itself, and embassies were sent out by the Senate to try to prevent this. Musonius attached himself to one of the missions and went among the Flavian soldiers urging them to peace. He was threatened by violence and withdrawn by his friends. Tacitus regarded this courageous act as 'untimely philosophy', in spite of the fact that the official leader of one of the delegations, no less a person than the friend of Thrasea, Arulenus Rusticus, now praetor, was also wounded, and that another delegation consisting of the Vestal Virgins had no better success.

The attitude of Lucan was different. His quarrel with Nero may have stemmed from trivial causes, but he went on to develop a theme of opposition to the emperor on better principles than literary differences. A fragment of his biography by Suetonius says that 'in the end he was almost the standard-bearer of the Pisonian conspiracy, full of threats and openly proclaiming the glory of tyrannicides'.

Lucan's uncompleted poem on the civil war between Caesar and Pompey (usually called the *Pharsalia*, though the original title was *De Bello Civili*) dates from the last years of his life. Only three books, presumably I–III, were published in the poet's lifetime. In book I there is an adulatory passage on Nero which may indicate that the poem was begun before his break with the emperor, but otherwise the philosophical background of the poem was entirely Stoic; Lucan, like his contemporary, the satirist Persius, had been a pupil of the philosopher Annaeus Cornutus. He rejected the whole divine apparatus of causation so characteristic of ancient epic, and accepted Stoic determinism. More important is an intense feeling of loss for the Roman Republic, and admiration for a vanished tradition. The rhetorical mode of expression may be unsympathetic to modern taste, but is entirely suitable to the presentation of these feelings in Stoic terms. Caesar is shown in word and deed with all the vices attacked by Stoicism, unbridled ambition and lust for power, a fierce and uncontrolled temper. Pompey on the other hand, though liable to vanity, ambition and fear, improved in character till his death. Above all Cato is the true Stoic hero. He is not moved by any passion in spite of the collapse of his cause. Lucan here parts company with Seneca; Cato plays his part in the drama of the dying Republic regardless of whether the outcome is inevitable or not. He is apostrophized, 'Behold the true parent of his country, worthy indeed of Roman worship, by whom no one will be ashamed to swear and whom, if Rome ever stands again with unbowed neck, she will make a god' (*Pharsalia* IX, 601–604). Whether the poem would have continued to the assassination of Caesar is not clear, but even in the existing books there are a number of references to Brutus the tyrannicide. It can thus be seen that whereas Seneca in his final years and Musonius implied, if they did not fully advocate, a withdrawal from politics and a concentration on the moral philosophy of the Stoics, Lucan, in his surviving poem, was committed to a viewpoint which could and did lead to outright opposition to Nero, and perhaps to Republicanism.

Even a minor figure like Persius had some importance because his few poems were widely admired by the end of the first century. He died in 62 before the age of 30. Like Musonius, he was of equestrian rank and from

Etruria, his home being Volaterrae. Persius' Stoic orthodoxy was notable, and it is significant that although he
knew Seneca, he was not won over as many young men
were. Five of his six Satires are on themes dear to the
Stoics. Only the first may have been directly offensive,
as it was an attack on the literary amateurism and poor
taste of the day; its terms could certainly have included
the Neronian circle.

The Fall of Nero

THE surviving part of Tacitus' narrative breaks off with the death of Thrasea and we lack his accounts of Nero's tour of Greece and of his overthrow. Many of the details of this dramatic event are accordingly not very clear. Suetonius has an extended account of Nero's last days, but it is highly coloured and sentimental in the manner of an ancient novel; nevertheless it corresponds in some details with the fragmentary account in Dio.

While Nero was in Greece from late 66, attacks on prominent men continued both in Rome itself and at Nero's court. It was in Nero's last years that the much criticized *delatores* (private prosecutors) again became powerful. The use of prosecutions as a political weapon in the struggle for personal or factional power had a long history even in Republican times. The practice was sanctioned because enforcement of the Roman criminal law depended for the most part on prosecutions by private individuals rather than by the state. Under the Empire, *delatores* came under a cloud when ambitious men found it easy to acquire wealth and honours by playing on the suspicions of the emperors and undertaking prosecutions of persons for treason, where acquittals were unlikely. This naturally only applied to important cases in Rome and Italy. A rather artificial distinction had to be drawn between those who undertook prosecution in the public interest and those who, particularly in treason cases, did so through ambition and greed. Under Nero, up to 66, we hear only of Eprius Marcellus and Cossutianus Capito, accusers of Thrasea. Subsequently the most important was a young man, Aquilius Regulus. His victims were all of noble families: M. Licinius Crassus Frugi, consul in 64 and brother of Galba's heir and colleague; an elderly consular, Q. Sulpicius Camerinus, and his son; and Sergius Cornelius

Salvidienus Orfitus, consul in 51. It may be supposed that they were all removed because their social origins made them potential figureheads of conspiracies, like Piso.

Up to 66 no governors in command of armies and indeed no provincial governors in office had attracted Nero's suspicions. But in late 66 or early 67 Corbulo was summoned to Greece, and as soon as he disembarked received the order to die. He is said only to have made the ambiguous remark, 'I deserved it.' This can certainly mean that he regretted his long loyalty to Nero, but it is difficult to separate his death from the conspiracy of Vinicianus discovered at Beneventum in 66. Though no details are known, this must derive its name from Annius Vinicianus, Corbulo's son-in-law, and perhaps aimed to replace Nero with Corbulo. Vinicianus' brother Annius Pollio had been exiled on grounds of complicity in the Pisonian conspiracy—and Pollio's wife was the imprudent daughter of Barea Soranus. The father of the two brothers, L. Annius Vinicianus, had been a leading member of the conspiracy which removed Gaius, and had then instigated the revolt of Camillus Scribonianus against Claudius in 42. There was thus a family record of hostility to emperors. About the same time, two brothers who were famous for their mutual affection were likewise summoned to Greece where they were ordered to commit suicide. They were Scribonius Rufus and Scribonius Proculus who were, or had recently been, commanders of Upper and Lower Germany respectively. Nothing is known against the Scribonii except their noble origin; they seem to have been connexions of Sulpicius Camerinus and Licinius Crassus Frugi, likewise victims in this year.

When Cestius Gallus, governor of Syria, died in 66, he was replaced by Licinius Mucianus, whose family and origin are unknown but were apparently modest. Vespasian, placed in charge of the Jewish war from early 67, Fonteius Capito and Verginius Rufus, who replaced the Scribonii in Lower and Upper Germany, were likewise all of undistinguished family. These appointments reflect the fear of the old nobility now felt by Nero and manifested in the numerous executions. It was not so much that emperors were always fearful of army commanders as such; up to 68 there had been only one revolt by such a man, that of Camillus Scribonianus in 42. It had been disastrous and his troops returned to their imperial allegiance in a few days. On the other hand, there had been the successful assassination of Gaius in Rome, and other plots which could easily have succeeded. Furthermore, Verginius, Vespasian and the rest came from a social milieu similar to that of a number who had taken part in, the Pisonian conspiracy, and Vespasian had been a friend of Thrasea and Soranus; their loyalty could not be taken entirely for granted. But it was quite clearly held that only men of the highest social origin could challenge the Julio-Claudian family so long entrenched in the imperial position. Nero therefore began to exclude them from army commands in case they were tempted to act in support of conspiracies hatched in Rome, while at the same time striking down nobles who seemed particularly dangerous.

Seneca had once said to Nero, 'However many men you kill, you can never kill your successor'; the triumph of the unexpected came when a revolt was begun by a provincial governor who had no legion at all, and was continued by another who had only one. During Nero's absence in Greece—he was away from the city longer than any emperor since Tiberius had retired to Capri—hostility to the régime continued to grow. His freedman Helius, whom he had left in effective charge in Rome, several times wrote advising him to return because of the movement of opinion. When Nero failed to respond, Helius finally hurried to Greece in person and at last persuaded Nero to return. He may well have had information of the plot which was in the making. Nero arrived in Naples early in 68 and then moved to Rome. He had learned nothing; he was hailed by the crowds, in quasi-divine terms suitable for the Hellenistic world rather than Rome, and his entry into the city and procession to the Capitol as a victor in the Greek games was a parody, probably deliberate, of the traditional Roman triumphal procession by victorious generals. He was soon back in Naples, and it was there between 19 and 23 March that he heard of the revolt in Gaul.

C. Julius Vindex was of praetorian rank, and the governor of, in all probability, Gallia Lugdunensis, though it is not impossible that he governed Gallia Narbonensis. He was a descendant of tribal chieftains in Aquitania and his father was probably a beneficiary of Claudius' introduction of Gallic notables into the Senate. He is described as courageous, daring and intelligent. Before openly rebelling, he had sought the participation of other governors; as governor of Gallia Lugdunensis he would have only a few hundred soldiers at his disposal (Narbonensis had none). His contacts, with one exception, informed Nero that a revolt was in the making. Vindex was, however, bound to go through with his venture in spite of the lack of support, once it was known. Early in March he threw off his allegiance and at the same time called on Servius Sulpicius Galba, governor of Hispania Tarraconensis, to accept the leadership of a revolt against Nero. Vindex was supported by the Aedui, Arverni and Sequani, all powerful tribes, and by the Roman colony of Vienna (Vienne) in Narbonensis, but he probably had more allies than this. He was opposed by other tribes, however; we know of the Treviri and the Lingones and the colony of Lugdunum (Lyon), the latter loyal to Nero because of his benefactions after a disastrous fire. Vindex's main strength was in the leaders of the tribes in his cause, and he promised Galba that he would have 100,000 men; in the event, some 20,000 fell when he was defeated, a substantial number which indicates how the Gallic notables could still call on the support of thousands of their clients.

The theme of the manifestos of Vindex was the liberation of the Roman world from a cruel and unworthy tyrant, 'not even a good lyre-player'. The coinage of both Vindex and Galba confirms this. Vindex's first issues had traditional motifs such as *SPQR* and *SIGNA P. R.*; one significant legend was *SALUS GENERIS*

HUMANI (Well-being of the Human Race); in his letter to Galba, Vindex had called on him precisely to be 'the Champion of the Human Race'. Subsequent issues in Gaul and Spain referred to 'Rome Reborn', 'Rome Restored' and the 'Liberty of the Roman People'. Most of these themes had precedents in Augustan and later coinage; their message in the context of Vindex's revolt was that a new emperor who would be in the true Roman tradition was available for formal confirmation by the Senate and People of Rome.

Galba was an elderly member of one of the few surviving families of the old Republican nobility; he was seventy-three, and had been a popular governor of Tarraconensis for eight years. In spite of his age, his candidacy could be justified in the circumstances by his past record, by the view that only a man of his standing had a chance of succeeding, and by his total contrast to Nero. He is said to have intercepted messages from Nero to his procurators to kill him, presumably for not denouncing Vindex. Whether he agreed to become the leader of the movement against Nero only after Vindex had rebelled and called on him publicly to accept the position, as the tradition held, may perhaps be doubted. He took as his title for the time being 'Legate of the Senate and People of Rome', thus demonstrating a formal adherence to constitutional practice, since imperial power had to be conferred at Rome. His proclamation took place at Nova Carthago (Cartagena) in Spain on 2 April; he was followed by his own legate, T. Vinius, by Salvius Otho, governor of Lusitania, and Caecina, quaestor of Baetica, but he had only the one legion of Spain, though he began to enrol another.

Nero appears to have taken no special steps when he heard of Vindex's revolt, supposing no doubt that it would be put down by Verginius Rufus, commander of the nearest army; only after Galba joined did he begin to act. Orders were sent for the recall of troops who had assembled for the expedition to the 'Caspian Gates'; legions were also summoned from Illyria, including XIV Gemina, on its way from Britain to the East, and which seems to have been in the Illyrian area; it was notable for its loyalty to Nero. He began to recruit a new legion from the fleet at Misenum and even, it is said, to levy among the Roman proletariat and slaves. Available troops were put under the command of Petronius Turpilianus and Rubrius Gallus and sent in the direction of Gaul. At the end of April Nero assumed a sole consulship, a traditional mark of an emergency.

Meanwhile Vindex had assembled his levies and was besieging Lugdunum. While he was thus engaged, Verginius Rufus marched with his three legions against Vesontio (Besançon) which had declared for Vindex. This happened at the beginning of May at the earliest. Verginius, with a battle-ready army only a few days' march from the area of Vindex's main support, had taken at least two months to react one way or the other. Although he subsequently resisted pressure from his own and other legions to make himself emperor, it seems that he temporized as long as he dared to see whether Vindex's movement looked like succeeding. Vindex and Virginius had a secret meeting and it was afterwards believed that they had agreed to work together. However, the two armies came into conflict because of lack of discipline and desire for plunder among the legionaries who, besides, despised the Gauls. Vindex and his levies were no match for the professional soldiers, and 20,000 were massacred. Vindex committed suicide. One version of events had it that immediately after the battle Verginius' troops tried to make him emperor and even threw down images of Nero, but that he refused and got the troops to agree to abide by the decision of the Senate and People of Rome; this would in any case have been treasonable. Under the Flavian emperors it was in the interest of Verginius to antedate his defection from Nero, and it is possible that the offer to Verginius was not in fact made till after the news of Nero's death reached the Rhineland.

The revolt of Vindex has been seen as a movement of Gallic nationalism, but there is little evidence for this view. The coinage of Vindex and the attitude of Galba, who repeated the slogans of Vindex and rewarded the Gallic tribes who had helped him while punishing his opponents, speak against it; the elder Pliny, only a few years later, called Vindex 'the champion of freedom from Nero'. It may be added that to talk of nationalism as a dynamic political force in the ancient world is an anachronism, with the recognized exception of the Jews. This is not to say that within the ranks of the supporters of Vindex there were not some whose attitudes were anti-Roman; during the turmoil in Gaul in the next two years there were Druid fanatics to prophesy the fall of Rome, and tribal notables willing to join with the Germans, their traditional enemies, in an assault on the Roman position in the Rhineland. They were limited, however, precisely to tribes who had opposed Vindex, which demonstrates the survival of strong local and tribal rivalries. Suggestions that the Gauls rose for independence for Gaul rather than freedom from Nero, where they are not due to rhetorical devices in the sources, may be due to Verginius. Though he was praised for refusing the throne, he could be criticized for bad discipline in his army (despite his prestige, nothing is known of his military record) and for being slow in support of Galba. Whatever the truth about Vesontio, he had certainly led his legions into Gaul in a threatening manner, and could excuse this by alleging that the movement of Vindex was a threat to his position on the Rhine. His epitaph, which was famous, was no doubt deliberately ambiguous: 'Here lies Rufus, who after defeating Vindex [*or* by the defeat of Vindex] claimed the Empire, not for himself, but for his country.'

When Galba received the news of the death of Vindex, he wrote to Verginius asking him to join in efforts to 'save the Empire and freedom of Rome', but then retired to the small town of Clunia in the interior of his province; his cause must have seemed hopeless. For Nero, however, news of the event seems to have brought no relief. Even if the story that Verginius had defected after Vesontio, without openly supporting Galba, is true, firm nerves and decisive action to put himself at the head of the Illyrian troops already moving towards Italy could have saved the emperor. But it was precisely at this point that Nero betrayed himself. No doubt the many stories of his alternating moods of euphoric optimism and wild panic lost nothing in the telling; it was said that he proposed to execute all exiles and all the Gauls in the city, and to poison the entire Senate; he would set fire to Rome (again?) and turn the wild beasts loose on the people; he would proceed unarmed to the soldiers and regain their loyalty by an appeal to their emotions, or go as a suppliant to Parthia or rule the east from Egypt. Whatever the truth, the situation slipped out of control; Clodius Macer, the legate of the African garrison, defected, and while putting out propaganda of a quasi-Republican type acted on his own account. Nothing is known of any activity by Rubrius Gallus or Petronius Turpilianus; the former may have been disloyal. In Rome, although Galba had naturally been outlawed, it was clear that substantial elements were waiting their opportunity.

This could only come with the defection of the praetorian guard. For reasons which are not known, Tigellinus played no part in the events of 68, and Nymphidius Sabinus appears as the more influential of the prefects. His role seems to have been underestimated in the sources, as if it was undesirable to admit the importance played in the fall of Nero by such a deplorable person, who was subsequently disloyal to Galba as well. He made common cause with the Senate and set about suborning the loyalty of his troops. Nero finally determined to leave Rome by sea, apparently for Egypt, on 8 June. The tribunes and centurions either refused or showed great reluctance to accompany him. During the night the unit on duty deserted. Nymphidius, accompanied by senators, went to the praetorian camp, and, after telling the soldiers that Nero had fled and promising a large donative, persuaded them to proclaim Galba as emperor. This was followed at once by decrees of the Senate declaring Nero a public enemy and Galba the new emperor.

Accompanied by only a few freedmen, Nero fled to the house of one of them, Phaon by name, about four miles from Rome. While there he heard of the Senate's decree and after some hours of terror stabbed himself in the throat with the help of his freedman Epaphroditus, as the soldiers sent to arrest him approached. The lurid story of his flight and last hours stresses the desertion of all but a few freedmen and women. Among the remarks remembered from his last hours, the most famous was, 'What an artist perishes in me,' too much in character to be seriously doubted. His death was not followed by scenes of savagery such as marked the death of a number of unpopular emperors and modern autocrats. His nurses and former mistress Acte were allowed to give him an expensive funeral at the tomb of the Domitii.

It was not so much the cruelty as the frivolity and ineptitude of Nero which led to his downfall. At the best of times cruelty is a relative term; for example, as understood by the Romans, it did not include the savage penalties of the cross, the beasts and the fire inflicted on criminal slaves and non-citizens. Emperors were charged with cruelty who were ruthless in the removal of members of their family and men whom they regarded as potential rivals, and also for sadistic enjoyment of the physical and mental sufferings of their victims. Nero could be accused on the former count; the latter played little part in the tradition, and Nero generally adhered to the convention which allowed a senator to commit suicide rather than suffer the indignity of execution.

It is not surprising that the personality and interests of Nero, so different from those of other emperors, were displayed in many an anecdote. Suetonius has a large number and they were doubtless in the sources used by Tacitus and Dio as well, though the former only retails a few. Most of them centred on his musical and theatrical pursuits and his sexual life, his wives, mistresses and eunuchs. It is often said that in this respect the historians merely provided what their readership required, but the notion that the private indulgences of even approved figures such as Augustus or Trajan should be concealed from posterity was alien to the Romans. The licence of autocratic power was enjoyed by the emperors as by the rulers of seventeenth- and eighteenth-century Europe if not indeed of later times as well. It must be admitted, however, that Neroniana lost little in the telling, and were not difficult to manufacture. This applies even to quoted remarks of the emperor, although *ipsissima verba* are generally supposed to resist the ravages of time better than anecdotes.

For example, it was said that he looked at his mother's corpse and said, 'I did not know that I had such a beautiful mother' (Tacitus doubts this); that when the head of Rubellius Plautus was brought to him he remarked, 'I did not know he had such a big nose,' and that when he saw the head of Faustus Sulla he laughed at its premature baldness. It may be suspected that these came from the biographies of his victims and served to illustrate the theme of Nero as a callous tyrant. Another example concerned the fire of Rome. Someone quoted a well known line from a Greek poet: 'When I am dead, may the earth be consumed with fire,' to which Nero replied, 'No, when I am alive,' and set about his activities as an incendiary. Quite apart from the responsibility for the fire, faith in the attribution of the remark is weakened by the fact that the quotation is attributed also to Tiberius, in a fit of gloomy misanthropy. Perhaps those to do with his art are the most likely to be true; before he finally ventured to appear in public he quoted the Greek proverb, 'No one has any regard for music they have not heard,' and when dining in public at Naples addressed the bystanders, 'When I have had a drink I'll give you a rousing song.' A celebrated remark referred to what he would do if he lost the Empire: 'My art will support me.' His last words show him obsessed to the end by his theatrical mania.

For an emperor to survive the alienation of the upper class was difficult; Domitian failed, like Nero and Gaius, though he lasted longer. Nero had little compensating strength; he was popular among the proletariat of Rome, but this body counted for more when it was hostile than when it was favourable to an emperor; his popularity in the Greek world, though real, was likewise of little practical value. In his later years, financial pressure on the provincials was doubtless considerable, and we hear of the unpopularity of his taxes and of his procurators in connexion with the movement of Vindex and Galba, but there was no general hostility on which these two could rely. In general, provincials were powerless to do anything other than obey the wielders of power, legitimate or usurpatory. They were not disloyal to Rome, but did not, or could not, show much effective enthusiasm for a particular ruler.

Nero's neglect of the army also played its part, but it should not be exaggerated. He is said to have allowed the pay of the soldiers and the provision for discharged veterans to get into arrears. If widespread, this would have been very serious, but it is only reported by Suetonius who notoriously generalized from individual instances. On the whole, there is little evidence that Nero was not popular among the soldiers, and some units (e.g. XIV Gemina) are known to have been enthusiastic for him. In fact, the notion that the legionaries, as opposed to their officers, frequently played a part in the rise and fall of emperors is illusory for this period. The legionaries of the army on the Rhine were admittedly enthusiastic for Vitellius, but the movements of 69 were all plotted and inspired by provincial governors, commanders of legions and the legionary tribunes and centurions. On the other hand, Nero's failure ever to visit an army was important in a negative sense. It made things worse in the crisis as he simply had no idea how to act; if he had acquired a military reputation, or even some prestige, like Claudius, there might never have been a venture like that of Vindex.

One of the cherished beliefs of Roman moralists was that the country towns of Italy preserved the sober and respectable habits which had once characterized the citizens of Rome but which had now died out in the city.

Tacitus saw an example in the decline of Nero's authority. The repetition of Neronia in 65 was popular with the city masses. But, says Tacitus, 'those who had come on official or private business from distant country towns in Italy where the strictness of ancient manners was retained, and from distant provinces, without experience of such decadence, could not bear the sight of an emperor on the stage' (*Annals* XVI, 5). The participation of such men in the Pisonian conspiracy and in the later opposition gives some support to Tacitus' view.

The first day of a new principate is the best, it was said, and there is no reason to doubt that at the fall of Nero there was enthusiasm in Rome among wider sections of the people than the Senate, but it was not universal. Tacitus differentiates:

> The senators were happy and at once used their new freedom of speech the more freely since they had an emperor who was still absent; the most important of the knights were next to the senators in feeling satisfaction; the respectable part of the people, attached to the powerful families, and the clients and freedmen of the condemned and exiled, were full of hope. But the base plebs, addicted to the circus and the theatre, and the worst of the slaves, and those who had wasted their money and were maintained by the emperor, to his own disgrace, were resentful and open to rumour. The praetorians, long accustomed to their oath to the Caesars, had been led to depose Nero by diplomacy and pressure rather than their own wish. . . . (*Histories* I, 4–5.)

Some of his freedmen were killed, mostly by mob violence, but the number was perhaps not large. Only one senator, Petronius Turpilianus, was killed for his association with Nero, and his death made Galba unpopular. In 69 and 70 some of the delators were prosecuted, but with little success. The same phenomenon is observable after the death of Domitian; it was considered bad form to rake over the past once a detested emperor was dead.

But it was not long before some regret for Nero was felt. In Rome his tomb was honoured with flowers for many years, from time to time his images were displayed, and edicts circulated in his name as if he were about to return. In 69 Otho found it worthwhile to try to win some popularity in the city by claiming to follow in Nero's footsteps after the gloomy and disappointing Galba; among other things he thought of marrying Statilia Messalina. Vitellius also tried to gain credit from his former close association with Nero. But it was in the East that the memory of Nero remained vivid. To the Greeks in Greece itself and no doubt also to educated Greeks everywhere, the 'liberation' of Achaea was important not only because it was symbolic of the concern of the first philhellene emperor and because it appealed to the nostalgic pride of the educated classes, but precisely because it lasted such a short time, being rescinded by Vespasian; they never had much chance to complain about its lack of reality. So Plutarch was able to regard it as Nero's one good deed that 'he freed the race of men that is the best and most dear to the gods of all the subjects of the Empire' (*Moralia*, 567F); Pausanias somewhat later agreed and in the third century Philostratus, who also had high praise for the projected canal through the Corinthian isthmus.

More than this, the obscure circumstances of his death provoked many rumours, and the belief grew up in the East that he was still alive. Dio Chrysostom wrote (under Trajan) that 'even now all long for him to be alive; indeed, many actually think he is still alive' (*Orations* XXI, 9 and 10). No less than three pretenders to the name of Nero appeared before the end of the century. The first, in 69, a slave or freedman, gathered some deserters and seized the Aegean island of Cythnos, killing the merchants there and arming the slaves. He was soon put down, but Tacitus says that Achaea and Asia were terrified, no doubt by the servile nature of the movement and the prospect of civil war. Under Titus another appeared, again similar in appearance and musical accomplishments to the dead emperor. He attracted a number of followers in Asia Minor and finally crossed the Euphrates into Parthian territory where his identity was soon discovered, though not before the Parthians had made some threatening gestures to restore him. Finally an impostor appeared in 88 who also fled to Parthia; it was with some difficulty that the Parthians were prevailed upon to hand him over. Their attitude was significant; they cherished the memory of Nero, and rightly in view of the Armenian settlement which was in their favour. They were, however, determined to maintain peace with the succeeding dynasty, and did not indulge in more than token gestures when the pretenders appeared.

Belief in the return of Nero entered still more humble circles, but with different implications. The Jews, embittered by the destruction of their country and the centre of their religion, continued to hope for divine vengeance on the Roman Empire, and from time to time prophecies of this, related to contemporary events, circulated among them. One such foretold that at the time of the eruption of Vesuvius (79), 'the exiled man of Rome, lifting a mighty sword, will cross the Euphrates [from Parthia] with many tens of thousands'. This no doubt refers to the pretender under Titus; the Jews hoped against all experience for Parthian support. The belief also existed among the early Christians, for whom Nero was known as the first persecutor; he appears in apocalyptic writings as the precursor of Antichrist at the end of the world.

A famous passage in Tacitus, one of the few in which he speaks directly, makes a favourable comparison between his own age and the past. He believed there had been an important change in the whole tone of Roman society in his own lifetime. Ostentatious luxury, which had run riot for a century since the victory of Augustus at Actium, had declined after the death of Nero. (Tacitus clearly thought that Augustus' measures to improve Roman society had had little effect.) The change was partly due to the liquidation of the richest nobles, which induced prudence in the rest. But, at the same time:

numerous self-made men admitted into the Senate from Italian towns and even from the provinces brought frugal domestic habits, and, though by luck or hard work many of them became rich later, they did not change their ideas. No one did more to promote simplicity than Vespasian, with his old-fashioned way of life; for deference to the emperor and the wish to imitate him were more effective than legal penalties and threats. It may, however, be the case that not only the seasons of the year but everything, including social change, moves in cycles. Not that earlier times were better than ours in every way—our own age has produced moral and intellectual achievements for our descendants to copy. (*Annals* III, 55.)

This naturally applied primarily to the upper class in Rome and Italy.

A notable example of the new type of senator (which included Tacitus himself) was his friend the younger Pliny. The latter's correspondence, which contains some indications of the wholesome life of the towns of his beloved northern Italy and hints of disapproval of individuals of the Neronian era, reveals the unostentatious way of life and sensible and well meaning attitudes of himself and many contemporaries. Again, when the satirist Juvenal was seeking examples of sophisticated vice, he turned back naturally to the age of Nero. What has been called 'Flavian morality' had its precursors in the principate of Nero, just as elements of Victorian morality were visible under the Prince Regent. One example was the agricultural writer Columella, another the elder Pliny.

There can be little doubt that Tacitus was correct in his belief in a change and in the reasons for it. Vespasian's abandonment of the Golden House, the most notorious example of Neronian extravagance, symbolized the whole process. The standards set by the emperors were important, and those who followed the short-lived emperors of 69 all came from precisely the circles praised by Tacitus—Vespasian from Italy, Trajan, Hadrian and Marcus Aurelius from Spain and

Antoninus from Gaul. Perhaps Titus had a different outlook from his father, but Domitian paraded a severe morality. The emperors from Vespasian to Marcus were in some ways all in the same mould, unlike the Julio-Claudian successors of Augustus, all markedly individual. The death of Nero brought to an end a dynasty which had links of blood and attitude with the great noble houses of the Republican era; now there were hardly any left, and those unimportant. The success of the new emperors depended much more on their abilities and conscientiousness. Although the monarchic character of the principate became ever more pronounced, no other dynasty achieved the prestige, or lasted half as long, as the Julio-Claudian.

The new situation did not immediately bring about the end of Stoic criticism, but it was confined to an ever narrowing circle and after a brief recrudescence under Domitian it ceased altogether. There were several reasons for this. One was the shock of the civil wars of 69. There was much destruction and slaughter, and Italy had suffered most; the sack of Cremona was particularly atrocious, there had been fighting in the streets of Rome, and the Capitol itself had been destroyed. It might be asked whether the removal of Nero was not paid for with too high a price. Furthermore, it nearly all happened again when Domitian was assassinated; for nearly two years there was a very real danger of civil war until the elderly Nerva designated Trajan as his successor.

There was also the fact that the events of 69 had exposed the Empire to external danger. Some German auxiliaries in the Rhine armies had revolted, and their fellow-tribesmen, with some disaffected Gallic tribes, had destroyed the whole Roman position on its most important frontier; it was restored with great difficulty by Vespasian's general Cerealis. The dependence of the Roman Empire itself on stable internal conditions was demonstrated, and the lesson of the civil wars at the end of the Republic learned again. This deepened the dilemma of those who opposed various features of the principate, if not the institution itself. Tacitus is an example of a man who saw that the existence of the Empire was bound up with the stability of the principate, but who never really became reconciled to the fact that this meant 'putting up with bad emperors while praying for good ones'. The more men became convinced of the unique greatness, even the eternity, of the Roman Empire, as they did in the second century, the more this became true. Thus Tacitus, who knew all the arguments that could be used to justify the system and to condemn the unreality of those who opposed it, did no more than hint at criticism of Thrasea; his deepest feelings, though not his intellect, were on Thrasea's side.

Finally, whereas violent opposition to Nero was perhaps inevitable in the end, given the evolution of the Julio-Claudian principate and the personality of Nero himself, opposition was less reasonable under later emperors. It was true that Domitian fell out with the Senate, but the whole trend of government from Vespasian onwards claimed the support of the upper classes not only in Rome and Italy but in the whole Empire, as knights and senators were recruited from an ever widening area. Successive emperors, without diminishing their powers in the smallest degree, found it worthwhile to keep on good terms with the upper classes, though this is not to say they governed exclusively in their interest. To this extent the decline of opposition was a capitulation to the emperor, since all depended on his personal characteristics. This, needless to say, is the characteristic of 'benevolent despotism'. A succession of rulers who were serious in their approach to government, respectful of the rights of property and tolerant of the prejudices, however outworn, of others, reinforced the political necessity. Stoicism could resume the theme of the just ruler; the younger Pliny's panegyric on Trajan has its senatorial veneer but differs little in essentials from the traditional Stoic view. Thrasea's circle had its paradoxical triumph in the second century; it was Q. Junius Rusticus, consul in 133 and 162, and grandson of Thrasea's friend Arulenus Rusticus, who introduced, or rather converted, the young Marcus Aurelius to Stoic philosophy, and thus played his part in providing the Empire with its philosopher-emperor. We may therefore see in the Stoic opposition to Nero the last protagonists, in however limited a form, of the classical Republic. For over a thousand years to come, monarchy, Roman or Germanic, was the unquestioned form of government throughout Europe.

Select Bibliography

Although Nero's principate as a whole has been handled by few scholars (the last extensive treatment in English was B. W. Henderson, *The Life and Principate of the Emperor Nero*, Methuen, 1903, which is now inevitably outdated, particularly in its manner of treatment), certain aspects of it have been thoroughly discussed in specialist periodicals. The following is only a brief selection of the more important books and articles published in English on some of the topics covered in this book.

Chapter 1
Translations of Tacitus' *Annals*, Suetonius' *Lives of the Caesars* and Josephus' *Jewish War* are available in the Penguin Classics series; a translation of the Neronian books of Dio Cassius is in the Loeb Classical Library (Heinemann; New York, Harvard University Press).

R. Syme, *Tacitus*, 2 vols, London and New York, Oxford University Press, 1958. An almost inexhaustible mine of information on all aspects of Tacitus.

G. B. Townend, 'The Sources of the Greek in Suetonius', *Hermes* LXXXVIII (1960), pp 98–120.

G. B. Townend, 'Traces in Dio Cassius of Cluvius, Aufidius and Pliny', *Hermes* LXXXIX (1961), pp 227–248. Argues for the sobriety of Pliny's work and the more sensational nature of Cluvius Rufus.

A. Momigliano, 'Literary Chronology of the Neronian Age', *Classical Quarterly* XXXVIII (1944), pp 96–100.

Chapter 3
A. M. Duff, *Freedmen in the Early Roman Empire*, New York, Barnes and Noble, 1928; reprint, Cambridge, Heffer, 1958. Includes an account of freedmen in the administration.

Chapter 5
R. S. Rogers, 'Heirs and Rivals to Nero', *Transactions of the American Philological Association* LXXXVI (1955), pp 190–212.

SELECT BIBLIOGRAPHY

Chapter 6
A. N. Sherwin-White, *Roman Society and Roman Law in the New Testament,* London and New York, Oxford University Press, 1963.
P. A. Brunt, 'Charges of Provincial Maladministration under the Early Principate', *Historia* X (1961), pp 189–223.

Chapter 7
H. I. Bell, 'The Economic Crisis in Egypt under Nero', *Journal of Roman Studies* XXVIII (1938), pp 1–8.
E. G. Turner, 'Tiberius Julius Alexander', *Journal of Roman Studies* XLIV (1954), pp 54–64. A study of the career of this important prefect of Egypt.
P. A. Brunt, 'The Fiscus and its Development', *Journal of Roman Studies* LVI (1966), pp 75–91.

Chapter 8
D. R. Dudley and G. Webster, *The Rebellion of Boudicca,* Routledge; New York, Barnes and Noble, 1962. Exhaustive treatment, but some of the views are dubious.
E. Birley, 'Britain under Nero' in *Roman Britain and the Roman Army,* Kendal, Titus Wilson, 1954.
M. Hammond, 'Corbulo and Nero's Eastern Policy', *Harvard Studies in Classical Philology* XLV (1934), pp 81–104.
S. G. F. Brandon, *Jesus and the Zealots,* Manchester University Press, 1967; New York, Scribner, 1968. A controversial book, containing a full account of the events leading to the destruction of Jerusalem

Chapter 9
M. P. Charlesworth, 'Nero: Some Aspects', *Journal of Roman Studies* XL (1950), pp 69–76. Discusses Nero's artistic enthusiasms and his reputation in the Greek world.
E. M. Sandford, 'Nero and the East', *Harvard Studies in Classical Philology* XLVIII (1937), pp 75–103. A survey of Greek and Oriental influence (probably exaggerated) on Nero.

SELECT BIBLIOGRAPHY

Chapter 10
W. Macdonald, *The Architecture of the Roman Empire,* New Haven, Yale University Press, 1965.
W. H. C. Frend, *Martyrdom and Persecution in the Early Church,* Oxford, Blackwell; New York, Doubleday (paperback) and New York University Press, 1965.

Chapter 12
Ch. Wirszubski, *Libertas as a Political Idea at Rome during the Late Republic and Early Principate,* Cambridge and New York, Cambridge University Press, 1950.
M. P. Charlesworth, *Five Men,* Martin Classical Lectures, 1936. Contains a sympathetic account of Musonius Rufus.
C. E. Lutz, 'Musonius Rufus, the Roman Socrates', *Yale Classical Studies* X (1947), pp 3–147.
J. M. C. Toynbee, 'Dictators and Philosophers in the First Century A.D.', *Greece and Rome* XXXVIII (1944), pp 43–58.

Chapter 13
P. A. Brunt, 'The Revolt of Vindex and the Fall of Nero', *Latomus* XVIII (1959), pp 531–559.
G. E. F. Chilver, 'The Army in Politics, A.D. 68–70', *Journal of Roman Studies* XLVII (1957), pp 29–35.
C. M. Kraay, 'The Coinage of Vindex and Galba', *Numismatic Chronicle* IX (1949), pp 129–149.

INDEX

The names of Emperors are in capitals

Main entries are in italic figures

177

178

179